# LOIS HOLE'S
# TOMATO
# FAVORITES

# Lois Hole's
# Tomato
# Favorites

*with*
## Jill Fallis
*Photography by*
## Akemi Matsubuchi

LONE
PINE

We have made every effort to correctly identify and credit the sources of all photographs, illustrations and information used in this book. Lone Pine Publishing appreciates any further information or corrections; acknowledgment will be given in subsequent editions.

### The Publisher: **Lone Pine Publishing**

| | | |
|---|---|---|
| #206, 10426–81 Avenue | 202A 1110 Seymour Street | Redmond Way, #180 |
| Edmonton, Alberta, | Vancouver, B.C., | Redmond, Washington, |
| Canada T6E 1X5 | Canada V6B 3N3 | USA 98052 |

Hole, Lois, 1933–
  Lois Hole's tomato favorites

(Lois Hole's gardening guides)
ISBN 1-55105-068-4

1. Tomatoes. 2. Cookery (Tomatoes) I. Fallis, Jill, 1960– II. Title. III. Title: Tomato favorites. IV. Series: Hole, Lois, 1933– Lois Hole's gardening guides.
SB349.H64 1996635'.642        C95-911163-8

*Senior Editor:* Nancy Foulds
*Project Editor:* Jennifer Keane
*Cover & Design:* Bruce Timothy Keith
*Production & Layout:* Bruce Timothy Keith, Greg Brown
*Printing:* Quebecor Jasper Printing Inc., Edmonton, Alberta, Canada
*Prepress:* Elite Lithographers Co. Ltd., Edmonton, Alberta, Canada
*Photography, including cover:* Akemi Matsubuchi

*Additional Photography*: **9a** Terry Bourque; **11c** Courtesy of David Tarrant; **16** Jim Hole; **17a** Courtesy of the Tomato Bank; **17b** Courtesy of Flying Tomato, Inc.; **63b, 145** Valerie Hole; **31, 74b** Courtesy of Brian Smith, Woodlea Nurseries; **32** (cartoon) Malcolm Mayes; **43a** Courtesy of Bradley County Pink Tomato Festival; **43b** Courtesy of Leamington District Chamber of Commerce; **43c & d** Courtesy of Reynoldsburg Tomato Festival; **60a** Courtesy of Petoseed; **71** Merle Prosofsky; **74a** Courtesy of PanAmerican Seed; **101a** Kharen Hill; **101b** Chris Van Huysse; **104b** Christopher Lemay; **106c** Jill Fallis; **116b** Courtesy of Mark Cullen; **126** Claudia Kronenberg; **154** Courtesy of Stokes Seeds Ltd.; **155a** Courtesy of The Original Tomato Company; **155b** Canapress Photo Service (Denis Doyle); **158, 159, 161, 163** Alberta Agriculture, Food and Rural Development, Crop Diversification Centre - South, Brooks, Alberta

The publisher gratefully acknowledges the support of Alberta Community Development, the Department of Canadian Heritage and the Canada/Alberta Agreement on the cultural industries.

'If you have eaten a tomato before a
test, you will have good luck.'
—folklore

---

# Acknowledgements

A special thanks goes out to all who love tomatoes, and to those who wrote letters to tell of their results and stories, and shared their favourite varieties, recipes and growing methods. I am especially grateful to the following people: Joyce Pearson, for her endless support and vast wealth of knowledge; Joan Green, for her special research skills; Jim Nau, for being a helpful source of information and for providing a tour of Ball Seed's trial gardens in Chicago; the many knowledgeable people at Alberta Agriculture; Don McBrien, for growing such beautiful tomatoes; the staff at our greenhouses, who contributed in so many different and wonderful ways; and to everyone who allowed our photographer, Akemi, into their yards and gardens.

# TABLE OF CONTENTS

# TOMATOES, TOMATOES, TOMATOES...

# Introduction

Tomatoes are the number one favourite vegetable, according to a 1994 Gallup poll. There are more than 30 million vegetable gardeners in North America, and 95 per cent of them grow tomatoes. Gardeners who grow no other vegetables are likely to have at least one tomato plant tucked in among their flowers, or growing in a pot on the patio.

Mom always grew lots of tomatoes in her garden. She made red tomato marmalade, which I absolutely loved. We used the ripest tomatoes to make home-made soup—and home-made tomato soup is still one of my favourite things to eat.

My friend Albina Yunick and I just loved to go out to Mom's garden when the tomatoes were ripe. We would take an old cup filled with sugar and dip the tomatoes in it. We'd eat two or three each, right there in the vegetable garden and warm sunshine. It's a childhood memory I will never forget.

Years later, after I had moved from Saskatchewan to Alberta, out to the farm with my husband Ted, tomatoes were the first plants I grew. People out for leisurely Sunday drives in the country could see our vegetable garden from the road, and would stop to ask if we had any vegetables for sale. Like all farm women, I always grew more vegetables than I needed, and was happy to sell the extras. It wasn't long before Ted and I decided to focus all our efforts on growing and selling vegetables. Our old red barn alongside the road with 'HOLE'S FARM' in two-foot-high white letters became a local landmark, and my vegetable garden grew larger every year.

We soon built a wooden greenhouse to give our tomato plants a head start on the season, and eventually replaced that with some larger, modern greenhouses.

*Tomatoes are among the most widely grown of all garden plants, edible or otherwise. For years, the tomato has been the only vegetable to make the top-ten list of best-selling bedding plants in North America.*

*Then and now: a shot of the old red barn (right), and an aerial of our greenhouses today (opposite).*

*Tomatoes were the first vegetables that we grew in our original greenhouse (above).*

After a couple of seasons we had close to 10,000 tomato plants inside one of the greenhouses, each plant producing about 10 pounds of vine-ripened tomatoes. There were more tomatoes than I had ever dreamed of having! People soon began to come out in the spring, asking to buy tomato seedlings and young plants to grow in their own gardens.

Over the years, growing and selling plants from our greenhouses became our major endeavour, and Ted and I no longer sell fresh vegetables. We still have our original garden near the house, which we now use to grow and test new vegetable varieties, and we dedicate one greenhouse for evaluating exciting new varieties of tomatoes, peppers and eggplant.

My mother and her twin sister Anne now live in the original farmhouse where Ted and I started out. Each fall, Mom, Auntie Anne and I gather in a steam-filled kitchen, with jars and pots and home-grown tomatoes, to preserve the season's bounty.

I want to share my experiences with you and make it easier for you to grow your own superb tomatoes. I will also share with you ideas from many professional growers, avid home gardeners and amateur 'tomato connoisseurs.' To complete the season, I've consulted with professional chefs and cooks. Their recipes are sure to entice.

Why are tomatoes so popular? I think partly because they are easy to grow, and in the kitchen, they are one of the most versatile vegetables. Tomatoes can be served at every meal: at breakfast, sliced as a side dish or chopped into scrambled eggs and omelettes; at lunch, in salads, sandwiches and soups; at dinner, to add flavour to meat, pasta and vegetable dishes of all description. To complement main courses, tomatoes can be served raw or cooked, canned, stuffed, sun-dried, juiced, pickled or made into any variety of tasty condiments.

## Home-Grown Tomatoes

*'...even people who don't like tomatoes eat them...'*

Even people who say they don't like tomatoes usually eat them in some form: as sauces or relishes on hamburgers, pizza, pasta or tacos, in soups, or as ketchup, salsa, barbeque and steak sauce. Salsa has recently overtaken ketchup as the number one sauce in North America; both are tomato-based.

Without a doubt, vine-ripened, home-grown tomatoes taste far better than the flavourless, mealy-textured tomatoes often found in grocery stores. But some home-grown tomatoes taste better than others. Taste really results from a combination of where, how and what: where you live, how well you care for your plants and what varieties you choose to grow. Even with garden tomatoes, not all varieties are equal—some simply have better flavour than others.

# Determinate or Indeterminate

*'...two basic types of tomato plant...'*

While there are hundreds of tomato varieties to choose from, there are just two basic types of tomato plant: determinate and indeterminate. They are easy to identify—determinate plants are bushy and fairly short, while indeterminate plants are tall and usually require staking. As the names suggest, determinate plants will grow to a certain point and then stop, while indeterminate plants, given the right conditions, will just keep growing. Beyond appearance, however, knowing the differences between the two types may help you decide which is best for your garden.

## DETERMINATE TOMATO PLANTS

- are often called 'bush tomatoes' because the plant is usually wider than tall.
- do not need pruning—pruning lowers yield!
- require more garden space than staked indeterminate plants.
- grow well in a cage.

## INDETERMINATE TOMATO PLANTS

- grow tall and require stakes or a trellis.
- should be pruned.
- when staked, take up less garden space than determinate varieties.
- usually have heavier yields than determinate varieties.

*Determinate tomato plants are the result of a mutant gene, known to scientists as sp for 'self-pruning.' Plant breeders were overjoyed at this discovery, which enabled them to produce tomato plants ideally suited for commercial field production. The upright growth habit meant fruit was held off the ground without staking, so less work was required, and most fruit ripened at the same time, requiring fewer harvests. Home gardeners love these features too!*

*On indeterminate plants, the leader or central stem keeps growing until fall frost, while leaders on determinate plants eventually produce flowers.*

*Although a tomato plant is commonly referred to as a 'vine,' it is actually a sprawling plant incapable of climbing. The word 'vine' refers to the tendency of indeterminate varieties to put out long, trailing branches.*

## SEMI-DETERMINATE TOMATO PLANTS

* are an 'in-between' category.
* grow upright like indeterminate plants, yet are bushy and sturdy like determinate varieties.
* do not need pruning but should be staked or caged.
* most often have thick stems and rugose (crinkled), dark green foliage.

## My Favourite Tomato Is...

'One of my favourite tomatoes for the coast is Oregon Spring, which was bred especially for Northwest gardens. In a good season, it will produce an abundance of early-ripening fruit.'

*David Tarrant,
host of CBC TV's
'Canadian Gardener'*

*If you're lucky enough to have a farmers' market in your area, you can supplement your supply of tomatoes.*

## The Difference Between Tomato Varieties

*'...flavour...'*

*Hothouse tomatoes have the same amount of vitamin C as summer-grown field tomatoes. Field tomatoes that are picked green have less vitamin C and about half the vitamin A.*

## Commercial Tomato Varieties

Ted refuses to eat any tomato that is not garden-grown and hand-picked. He disdainfully calls the others 'hardware tomatoes,' because those varieties are bred primarily for shipping and long shelf-life, with tough skins that can withstand the rigours of mechanical harvesting.

Huge mechanical harvesters shake commercial tomatoes from their vines while they are still green, long before flavour compounds have fully developed. These tomatoes ride conveyor belts, are dropped into crates, and must be gassed with ethylene to induce rapid ripening. Ethylene— the same gas that tomatoes give off internally if allowed to ripen on the vine—essentially 'tricks' the green tomatoes into turning red, so they look ripe even though they do not taste ripe.

The story doesn't end there. Before tomatoes arrive at the store, they are graded, packed, and hauled in refrigerated trucks, then unpacked and placed on the shelves. It takes a pretty tough tomato to withstand that much handling, which is why most commercial varieties taste so different from garden varieties.

## Heirloom & Hybrid

To my mind, there are two major divisions of tomatoes: the old and the new. Heirloom tomatoes are old, old varieties from which seed is saved each year for the following season's crop. Hybrid varieties are the result of cross-pollination between two or more parent lines to create a new and improved tomato plant. Hybrid, to me, means high-tech. I like hybrid varieties best but the heirlooms unquestionably have their place.

## HEIRLOOM VARIETIES

- Heirloom varieties are so-called because often the seeds have been passed down in families for generations.

- Many heirloom varieties have superb flavour. They also have a greater range of size, shape and colour; most of the oddest-looking tomatoes are heirlooms.

- Heirloom varieties maintain gene pool diversity! They are extremely useful for plant breeders in giving new hybrid varieties a natural resistance to various viral, fungal and bacterial diseases. In this respect, their contribution is priceless.

- Unfortunately, many of the most interesting heirloom varieties mature late in the season.

- All heirloom varieties are open-pollinated; in other words, they are pollinated naturally, by wind and insects, and don't need human help. Their seed can be collected and cleaned in the fall, and planted the following spring.

The original wild tomato was tiny and had only two cells or cavities, as you would see if you sliced open a cherry tomato. A genetic mutation is believed to have resulted in large, bumpy, multi-celled fruit which were nurtured and developed by Central American farmers. Today's large, smooth-skinned fruit are mainly crosses between that mutation and the smooth-skinned cherry tomato.

## HYBRID VARIETIES

- Most of my recommended varieties are hybrids.

- Many new hybrid varieties have superb flavour and far higher yields than heirloom or older hybrid varieties.

- Plant breeders, by and large, are able to breed specific characteristics into hybrid varieties, including better flavour, early ripening, improved fruit-set at extreme temperatures, consistent fruit size, firmness, heavy yields, disease resistance, crack resistance and heavy protective foliage.

- You can save seed from hybrid tomatoes but keep in mind that some of the seed will not produce true to type—in other words, some of the resulting plants will not retain the best characteristics of their parents.

There are over 5,000 tomato varieties in all kinds of colours, shapes, sizes and tastes.

*Gardener Bruce Loowell favours the heirloom variety 1884.*

# Genetically Engineered Tomatoes

The first genetically engineered food approved for sale to U.S. consumers was the Flavr Savr tomato. It was launched with promises of having greatly increased shelf-life and year-round 'summertime flavour,' because of its ability to be harvested ripe rather than green, as are most commercial tomato crops.

Another genetically engineered tomato is in the early stages of test-marketing. With this one, scientists have apparently discovered a way to 'turn off' the ripening gene, suspending the tomato in a state of perfect ripeness. The tomato can then either be left on the vine for up to 60 days or picked immediately, lasting seven to ten days longer after being picked than other vine-ripened varieties. (The difference between the two is that Flavr Savr is genetically altered to control and block final softening, while in this one, it is the ripening that is controlled.)

Yet another genetically engineered tomato is in the works. It is supposed to have increased resistance to freezing, due to the inclusion of genetic material taken from fish!

*A tomato makes a refreshing snack after a workout for Jeff Robinson.*

The average length of time between transplanting and harvest is referred to as 'days to maturity.' I use 'days to maturity' as a guideline rather than a guarantee. These numbers can be misleading if your garden conditions differ from those used in the test garden. Weather makes a difference and conditions vary from garden to garden: in a summer that is cooler and cloudier than normal, harvest will be delayed; in an ideal setting—warm, sheltered and sunny—your plants may mature more quickly than expected.

'Days to maturity' is calculated using optimum temperature; with tomatoes, the range is from 21 to 24°C (70–75°F). If, during every single day of the growing season, the daytime and nighttime temperatures averaged 21°C (70°F)—say, 26°C (79°F) during the day and 16°C (62°F) at night—and all else was perfect, two months after planting you would be picking ripe tomatoes from a variety with 60 days to maturity. But every day with an average temperature below the optimum of 21°C (70°F) slows maturity; for every 1°C (3–4°F), add on several days.

For example, in Edmonton, Alberta, the average July temperature is 17.5°C (64°F), while in Detroit, Michigan, it is 22°C (72°F). Detroit gardeners can therefore expect maturity dates pretty much as listed, but Edmonton gardeners should tack on four to five days per degree, bringing the maturity dates to a total of at least two weeks later than those listed. My friend Dave Matthews, a gardening columnist who lives in Calgary, advises gardeners there to add a whole month, because of Calgary's high elevation and cool nights. If you want to figure out how to gauge maturity dates for your city, check with your local newspaper or weather office for the average monthly temperature for July.

# Days to Maturity  15

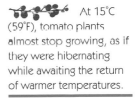 As a general rule, varieties that produce larger tomatoes produce fewer and are later-maturing.

At 15°C (59°F), tomato plants almost stop growing, as if they were hibernating while awaiting the return of warmer temperatures.

*Grow varieties that mature at different times to provide ripe tomatoes over a longer period.*

If you don't want to bother figuring it out, don't worry. Use my general rule to make it simple: consider from 50 to 60 days as 'early,' from 61 to 70 days as 'mid-season,' and more than 70 as 'late.' With early varieties gardeners in colder climates are guaranteed a harvest, with mid-season varieties they are almost assured, and with late varieties, they will usually have a harvest.

## The Best Home-Grown Tomatoes
*'...be willing to experiment...'*

When Ted and I began growing tomatoes for our market garden, we chose the varieties Bounty and Early Chatham, along with Starfire, Rocket and Manitoba. That was over 40 years ago; today, none of these varieties remains on our recommended list.

## Experimenting with New Varieties

Plant breeders are constantly improving existing varieties, and seed companies introduce new ones each year. Be willing to experiment in your own garden by growing at least one new variety every year—it adds fun to gardening!

Each year at our greenhouses, we test about a dozen new varieties; we recommend a new variety only if it has performed well in our garden. We reject many varieties—not because they are poor but because they do not show a significant improvement over those we already grow. Once in a while, however, we do discover a new one that is truly amazing. We then either add it to our recommended list or use it to replace an existing variety.

If you have had wonderful luck with a certain variety, I don't expect you to change—but I do hope you'll experiment a bit. Continue to grow your favourites, but also try at least one new variety, and preferably two. Never plant just one kind of tomato—live a little dangerously! Spend an extra couple of dollars on a tomato variety that you have never grown before. Don't be afraid to experiment with 'fringe' types; you could be pleasantly surprised.

*Alberta Agriculture's Paul Ragan evaluates various tomato varieties in the test fields at Brooks.*

I always recommend that if you have eight tomato plants, grow at least two varieties—but four would be even better. Remember that performance changes under different weather or growing conditions. A great variety may not fare so well in a cool, wet summer. If you had bad weather for your first attempt at growing a certain kind and you decided to give up on it, you could be missing out on something wonderful!

# TOMATO MANIA

**THE TOMATO** is the very visible logo of the Tomato Bank in Okayama City, Japan. Bank owners apparently believe that the tomato is a symbol of power, and the logo appears on everything from the bank's cheques to the pins and uniforms worn by staff. The staff even starts the day with a Tomato Song! The bank gives each new customer a colourful book filled with poems and short essays about tomatoes. The bank's mascot is—what else?—a giant tomato.

**IT'S A BIRD**, it's a plane … no, it's a flying tomato! A 7-storey-tall tomato floating 800–1000 feet (244–305 m) over the heads of people in the U.S. Midwest is not as shocking a sight as you might believe. Two Flying Tomato hot-air balloons are a promotion for Flying Tomato Pizza in a Pan, a 17-outlet chain with stores in Illinois, Ohio, Indiana and Texas, owned by brothers Ralph and Joe Tomato (who aren't really brothers—their real names are Ralph Senn and Joe Ream).

# STARTING TOMATOES FROM SEED

*'...tomato seeds need warmth too...'*

*Tomato seeds usually take 7–14 days to germinate inside a home, and 5–7 days to germinate inside a greenhouse.*

When selecting tomato seeds, be sure to check the number of 'days to maturity.' As a general rule, consider from 50 to 60 days as 'early,' from 61 to 70 days as 'mid-season,' and over 70 as 'late.' See pages 15 and 16 for more details.

Some gardeners find it extremely satisfying to raise plants from seed, others can't be bothered. Growing tomato seedlings is fairly easy to do, but it does require a bit of time, effort and a suitable location inside your home. In my climate, if you want to grow tomatoes from seed you have to start them indoors to give the plants a head start on the growing season—otherwise they won't mature before fall frosts.

Every year we grow tens of thousands of tomato plants from seed at our greenhouses. The first crop is sown in mid-February, and successive crops are sown at two-week intervals until the end of April. Over the past 40 or so years, we must have raised well over a million tomato seedlings.

Growing tomato seedlings is now second nature, but it wasn't always so. The first time Ted and I sowed tomato seeds, we just could not get them to sprout. After a month, Ted wanted to throw them away, but luckily we decided to wait just a few more days. Spring weather arrived, and the extra sunlight warmed the seedling flats, which had been sitting on cold, bare ground in our old greenhouse. Within days of the higher temperatures, tiny shoots poked their heads through the soil, and we learned a lesson that we will never forget: tomato seeds must have warm soil!

# How to Start Tomatoes from Seed

**1.**          **2.**          **3.**

*1) Fill a seedling flat to within a half-inch (1.3 cm) of the top edge with a good-quality seedling mixture (a potting soil with a high percentage of sphagnum peat moss and perlite). Do not use garden soil, because it tends to become hard and inhibits proper rooting of seedlings, and it may contain insects, disease, weed seeds or chemical residue.*

*2) Follow the general rule for seeding: sow no deeper than the thickness of the seed. I sprinkle the seeds onto the soil-filled flat and press them down gently.*

*3) Cover the seeds with a thin layer of fine, horticultural-grade vermiculite to prevent drying.*

**4.**          **5.**          **6.**

*4) Water just enough to moisten the soil. To avoid dislodging the seeds, use a misting bottle with a very fine spray, or a watering can with a seedling nozzle. Never allow the seedling mix to become dry. Both germinating seeds and seedlings are very intolerant of dry soil and often will die even if the soil becomes dry for only a short time. Cover the flat with a sheet of plastic wrap or a plastic dome to improve humidity.* **Remove the plastic immediately after seedlings emerge.**

*5) Tag each container with the date planted and the tomato variety. Place the flat on a heated table, heat register or even on top of your refrigerator. This 'bottom heat' warms the soil and promotes rapid germination. Check the progress twice daily, in the morning and again at night.* **Remove the flat from heat as soon as the seedlings begin to emerge!** *Move the flat to a location with lots of light. Tomato seedlings need very high light levels to grow properly. A south-facing window without blinds or curtains (which filter the light) is ideal. Use grow lights to enhance growth.*

*6) Transplant the seedlings into larger, individual containers once the first 'true' leaves appear. At this point, seedlings are usually about ½ to 1 inch (1.3–2.5 cm) tall. If your seedlings are a bit stretched, transplant them slightly deeper; roots will soon form on the buried portion of the stem. After transplanting, fertilize with a plant-starter fertilizer such as 10-52-10, at ¼ strength. Continue to do this once a week until you transplant outdoors. Before planting outdoors, be sure to harden-off your plants.* *See pages 33 and 34 for instructions on how to do this.*

🌱🍅 The normal germination rate for tomato seed is about 90%. If fewer of your seeds sprout, you are either doing something wrong or the seed is too old or of poor quality.

*A seedling's first leaves are rounded and called 'seed leaves' or 'cotyledons.' The second set of leaves are 'true leaves' and resemble leaves of a mature plant. Transplant tomato seedlings into individual containers when the first true leaves appear.*

# WHEN TO SOW

A general rule is to start seed indoors about six weeks before you plan to transplant plants into your garden. If you have a greenhouse, you can start as soon as you turn on the heat. (See pages 118 to 122 for tips on home greenhouses.)

# STORING SEED

- Because tomato seeds remain viable for four to ten years, you can sow a few seeds of different varieties and store the remainder of each packet for use in following years. It's a good idea to date your seed packets with the year purchased.

🌱🍅 A soil temperature of 26°C (79°F) is best for germinating tomato seed. Above or below that, germination will be poor—it will take longer and fewer seeds will sprout. Tomato seed will not germinate if soil temperature is below 10°C (50°F) or above 35°C (95°F).

- Seal seed packets by folding tops down several times, and place them inside a sealed container—I use an old coffee can with a plastic lid.

- Store them in a cool, dry place.

- Tomato seed from a seed packet looks different from seed saved from your own tomato plants, because it has been 'de-fuzzed.' Each tomato seed is naturally covered in tiny, fuzzy hairs, which commercial seed companies remove to make sowing easier and prevent seeds from sticking together. For directions on how to save seeds from tomatoes you have grown, see pages 131–132.

## Cooking With Tomatoes

Here are some helpful measurements:

- 2 large, 3 medium or 4 small tomatoes
  = about 1 lb. (454 g)
  = 2 cups, chopped
- 20–24 cherry tomatoes
  = 1 lb. (454 g)
  = 2 cups, chopped
- One 28-oz. can of tomatoes
  = approx. 3 lbs. fresh (1.2 kg)
  = 3 cups, chopped
- 1–1 ¼ lb. tomatoes
  = 2 cups peeled and chopped tomatoes
- 2–2 ½ lbs. tomatoes
  = 1 qt. peeled and chopped tomatoes
- 25 lbs. raw tomatoes yields approx. 10 qts. canned tomatoes

Use overripe tomatoes for cooking, in sauces and in salsa.

Tomatoes are much better in salads if they are peeled. It takes extra time, however, so I peel them only for special occasions. Add tomatoes to salads last, as salt and salad dressing draw out their juices.

It is not necessary to peel tomatoes before cooking—the skins actually add flavour to sauces or soups. If you dislike the look of tomato skins, which tend to split and curl up into slivers when cooked, just strain the sauce later.

Chop or slice tomatoes just prior to using them. Tomatoes lose much of their flavour and some nutrients within an hour of cutting.

How do restaurants make those nicely warmed, but still firm cherry tomatoes? They heat them for a couple of minutes on low in the oven, just as you would warm a plate before serving.

Add flair to plain tomato soup by sprinkling grated cheese on it and topping it with croutons.

# BUYING TOMATO PLANTS

*'...more questions than any other plant...'*

*It is best to buy tomato plants from a greenhouse or garden centre.*

Without a doubt, at our greenhouses at least, gardeners have more questions about tomatoes than any other plant! Though I sometimes wonder if they would ask as many questions when buying a car, I really enjoy these discussions. There are two important rules that I share with gardeners shopping for tomato plants: buy at least two varieties, and always buy healthy plants. My reward often comes at the end of the season, in the form of photographs, letters, phone calls or visits from people with beautiful, ripe tomatoes in hand. Those gardeners who bring along their prized tomato, however, are understandably just as anxious to take it with them when they leave!

## BEFORE YOU BUY

Here are some things to consider before you head off to your local greenhouse to shop for this season's tomato plants.

**1) What do you want to do with your tomatoes?**

- If you mainly want them for salads, then almost any type of tomato will do, from cherry to paste to slicers and huge beefsteaks.

- Some people like tomatoes big enough that a single slice covers an entire hamburger or a whole slice of bread. Choose a tomato in the large, extra-large or huge categories.

- If you like to can tomatoes or make a lot of sauces, then a paste tomato or a high-yielding slicer like Floramerica is your best bet.

*Stocky tomato plants are the best choice, but a tall, stretched plant like the one on the right will grow well if trench-planted (see page 103).*

- Those who just want a few tomatoes to nibble on may prefer a dwarf ornamental cherry tomato such as Tiny Tim, which can be tucked into a flower pot or windowbox.

## 2) Which size plant is best?

- No matter which size you choose, the best tomato plants are dark green, stocky and free of bugs.

- If you want the earliest tomatoes, and price is not the primary consideration, choose large, vigorous plants in big containers. If price is a big factor, then choose small, vigorous plants in small containers.

a) 4-pack or 6-pack (several plants in a single plastic container).

- This is the most economical choice, especially good for gardeners who grow lots of tomatoes.

- These plants are smaller, so your harvest of ripe tomatoes will be slightly later than if you had started with larger plants.

b) One plant in a 4-inch pot or pack.

- The plants are larger so they will mature faster. This is a good choice for the gardener with limited space or who wants to grow more than one variety.

- Although still inexpensive, your cost per plant is higher.

c) One plant in a 1-gallon pot.

- A tomato plant in this size pot should be starting to show flowerbuds or already have green fruit. It will mature about two weeks earlier than smaller sizes.

- Your cost per plant is higher.

*If you accidentally break the top of a young tomato plant, so that there are few leaves left, go out and buy a new plant so as not to delay your harvest. Keep the broken one, because it will still grow, but it will take such a long time to produce that it's like starting with a 2-inch-tall (5 cm) seedling rather than a larger plant.*

*For the ultimate in flexibility, grow a few different tomato varieties. Choose various types—perhaps a cherry and a paste along with a beefsteak or slicer—and also look for varieties that mature at different times, for an extended harvest season.*

d) One plant in a 5-gallon pot.

- This should be a very large plant already bearing green or occasionally ripe tomatoes. It is staked or caged, and does not need replanting—a plus for those who want an 'instant garden' or are getting a late start on the season.

- With a plant of this size, you can generally buy any variety, no matter what the number of days to maturity, and still be assured of harvesting ripe tomatoes. (See pages 15 and 16 for an explanation of 'days to maturity.')

- This is the most expensive way to buy tomato plants, but if you weigh the purchase price against the yield, you may just find out that the cost of tomatoes per pound is actually less!

### 3) Are the plants healthy?

- No matter how low the price, do not buy tomato plants of any size if they have broken tops, yellow or distorted leaves, bugs, or if they generally look very tall and stretched, unhealthy, pale or thin.

When shopping late in the season, buy the biggest tomato plants you can find. They'll cost more than smaller ones, but they are sure to produce, whereas smaller ones likely won't mature before fall frosts.

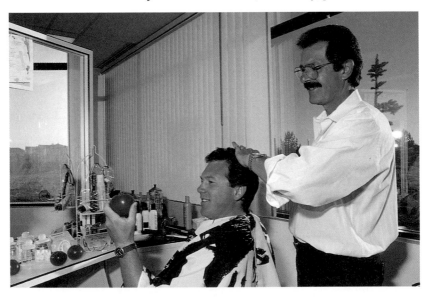

*Barber Marcel Chartrand's father thought he was crazy to spend extra money on a great big tomato plant, but the yield at the end of the season—enough tomatoes to fill two 5-gallon pails—convinced dad to buy his own big plant next year. Marcel shared the harvest with our greenhouse manager Dave Grice (seated) in thanks for his advice and growing tips.*

# Tomatoes Babiche

*'A scrumptious appetizer that is very fast to prepare.'*

—Joyce Pearson, Home Service Director, Blue Flame Kitchen, Northwestern Utilities Limited

6 medium tomatoes
seasoned salt & pepper
2-170 ml jars marinated artichoke hearts, drained
2-250 ml jars cocktail mushrooms, drained
½ cup mayonnaise
⅓ cup sour cream
1 tsp. curry powder
1 tsp. lemon juice
1 tbsp. instant minced onion
paprika
lettuce leaves

Scoop out each tomato leaving ¼-inch shell; sprinkle generously with salt and pepper. Fill with artichokes and mushrooms; refrigerate up to 6 hours. In a bowl, combine mayonnaise, sour cream, curry, lemon juice and onion; refrigerate. Just before serving, top each tomato with a generous spoonful of curry mixture. Place tomatoes on lettuce-lined plates. Pass extra sauce. Serves 6 as an appetizer or side salad with fish or chicken.

Note: for top quality, peel and chill tomatoes before stuffing.

# WHERE TO PLANT

*'...a location that resembles their homeland...'*

*'The Shivering Immigrant' is one of the more amusing names for tomatoes, but it really is a fairly accurate description: these heat-loving plants are native to South America. Imagine their shock at finding themselves in gardens where frost in June isn't as rare as we would wish! To keep tomato plants at their best, provide a location that mirrors their homeland: hot and sunny. A sheltered spot is even better, for wind not only cools things down but can slow tomato plants' growth. Always protect tomato plants from frost.*

## BEFORE YOU PLANT

- Tomatoes always do best in a warm, sunny, sheltered spot. A south-facing location near a wall is perfect.

- Never plant in 'frost hollows'—low-lying spots where cold air accumulates, particularly during cold nights. Plants in these areas are usually the first to be hit by frost.

- In raised beds, tomato plants mature more quickly and can often be planted slightly earlier, because the soil in raised beds warms faster than soil in open gardens.

- Wooden or brick walls reflect heat, which is great for tomatoes (see photo below), but white siding and stucco reflect excessive light, which can cause problems. Too much intense sunlight causes 'sunscald,' a condition characterized by pale greyish-white patches on fruit and leaves.

*A cartload of tomatoes is the innovative planting idea of Edmonton, Alberta gardener Lloyd Patriquin. The cart can easily be moved around to the sunniest part of his yard. This generous man grows about two dozen tomato plants each year, including ten hanging baskets of Tumbler, and gives away most of them to friends.*

- In a site sheltered from wind, tomato plants grow faster and larger, and will have more fruit that ripens quickly. Wind tends to cool plants and slow growth.

- Tomato plants have a relatively high tolerance to salt and do fine in seaside gardens or in beds near roadways or driveways where de-icing salt is used in winter. On a business trip to Israel, Ted visited a greenhouse near the Dead Sea, where water with a high salt content was used to water tomato plants. Ted said that the tomatoes tasted great.

# SOIL

- Tomato plants grow best in a soft, rich, well-drained soil that their roots can easily penetrate, and where nutrients are readily available. Water should percolate through easily, rather than pooling on the surface or draining away too quickly.

*This planting looks lovely, but yields might be higher if the tomato plant were given a site away from the tree, with less competition for moisture and nutrients.*

In Flin Flon, Manitoba, tomatoes grow—and flourish—1197 feet (365 m) below ground! A mined-out chamber in a zinc and copper mine owned by the Hudson Bay Mining and Smelting Company has been transformed into an underground garden, with computer-controlled light, humidity, water and fertilizer.

• Add lots of organic matter to your garden soil each year. Compost, peat moss and well-rotted manure are good choices.

• To quickly check the texture of your garden soil, scoop up a handful of moist soil and squeeze your hand into a tight fist. Now open your hand and have a look.

*Never add fresh manure to gardens, because it can burn plants. Well-rotted or composted manure is best.*

• If the soil stays in a ball, even when poked, and you can see the imprint of your fingers, then you have a clay soil—too hard for tomato plants to grow properly. Improve it by adding sand and lots of organic matter.

• If the soil falls away as you open your hand, it is a sandy soil—too quick to lose moisture and often low in nutrients. Add organic matter to improve it.

• If the soil stays compact but falls apart easily into small clumps when poked, then you are fortunate— you have the ideal garden soil.

## Ode To a Home-grown Tomato

The tomato's a fruit
So the experts say,
But most think of it
The other way.
Whether fruit or veggie
It's all the same,
The tomato's my favourite
Regardless of name.
. . . . . . . . . . . . .
—Patricia A. Bauer,
Wellfleet, Massachussets

Fruit or vegetable? Although we count the tomato among the most popular vegetables, technically it is a fruit. More surprisingly, it is most accurately classed as a berry: a fleshy fruit with many seeds embedded right into the juicy pulp.

Why then is there more confusion about the tomato than any other fruit, or vegetable? Probably because the tomato was always classed as a fruit until 1893, when a U.S. Supreme Court ruling instantly changed this most famous of fruits into a vegetable. This was after a six-year-long court battle in response to the tax department's attempts to collect levies on imported vegetables (fruit were exempt).

In his ruling, U.S. Supreme Court Justice Horace Grey explained: 'Botanically speaking, tomatoes are the fruit of a vine, just as are cucumbers, squashes, beans and peas. But in the common language of the people, whether sellers or consumers of provisions, all these are vegetables, which are grown in kitchen gardens, and which, whether eaten cooked or raw, are, like potatoes, carrots, parsnips, turnips, beets, cauliflower, cabbage, celery and lettuce, usually served at dinner in, with or after the soup, fish or meats which constitute the principal part of the repasts, and not, like fruits generally, as dessert.'

# Spaghetti Sauce

Living within a few steps of our greenhouses has its advantages, including the fact that our whole family always has a home-cooked meal for lunch. One of my favourite meals is also one of the simplest to prepare. Before I leave the house in the morning, I put an uncovered bowl of frozen spaghetti sauce in the oven at 250°F (121°C). When I come in at noon, it's nice and hot—all I have to do is cook the noodles and lunch is ready. (For those who don't have the luxury of coming home at noon, the bowls can also be reheated at 350°F [180°C] for about one hour.)

I never use a recipe to make spaghetti sauce. I just start with a basic tomato sauce and add lots of onions, celery, green, yellow and red peppers, chopped fresh basil, oregano and parsley, a drop or two of Tabasco sauce and a squirt of lemon juice. Cook about 30 minutes and serve. I often freeze extra spaghetti sauce right in an oven- and freezer-safe bowl for easier reheating.

 'All witches live on tomatoes.'
—folklore

# CONTAINER GARDENS

*'...almost any kind will do...'*

When we first started growing tomatoes in our greenhouses to sell at our farm market, we planted them in old, 5-gallon (23-litre) plastic buckets collected from various fast-food outlets in the city. One year we even grew tomatoes inside large, black plastic garbage bags, doubled-up, punctured at the bottom to allow for drainage and filled with soil mix. Most home gardeners likely prefer a more decorative choice, but this does prove that almost any kind of container will do the job!

## Tips for Container Gardens

- Tomatoes need about 1 cubic foot (0.028 m³) per plant when grown in containers.

- Fill containers with a top-quality, soil-less potting mix. The mix is typically a combination of peat moss, perlite, horticultural lime and slow-release fertilizer—often called 'potting soil' although it contains no soil at all! Garden soil should not be used because it tends to become rock-hard in containers.

- Don't fill containers right to the brim with soil. Leave a couple of inches (5 cm) of space from the brim to the soil surface. This makes it easier to water.

Good soil is like the foundation of a house; you want it to stand the test of time.

*Mix flowers with your tomatoes! A planter of impatiens, lobelia and Tumbler tomatoes makes an unusual and sensational display.*

- You don't have to use fresh potting mix every year, but it is a good idea. If you want to reuse old soil, then refresh it before planting. Remove it from the container, break up lumps, take out any old roots and add some fresh potting mix and a handful or two of slow-release granular fertilizer or bone-meal. Mix thoroughly before refilling your container.

- Almost any container will do, provided it has drainage holes and is big enough. Do not use anything made of clear plastic; in trying to grow away from the light, the roots will become stunted and the plants will not grow well.

- Do not use saucers underneath containers. The soil can become waterlogged and cause root-rot. If your plant has wilted, brown or yellow leaves, root-rot is the likely cause.

- Any tomato plant can be grown in a container, but some varieties are especially bred for that purpose. Dwarf ornamental varieties such as Tiny Tim look splendid in windowboxes or built-in planters, growing among a colourful assortment of flowers. The best variety to grow in hanging baskets is Tumbler. Once you see this plant grow, you'll know how it earned its name: its cascading branches are absolutely covered with small, sweet tomatoes that tumble over the sides of hanging baskets and tall planters.

- Container-grown tomato plants should be watered every day—even in cool, wet weather, because most of the rain is shed away from the pot by foliage. In periods of hot weather, you may need to water twice a day.

- Be sure to fertilize with a water-soluble fertilizer such as 20-20-20, in order to add the essential micronutrients that are lacking in most potting mixes. (See 'Fertilizing' on page 110.)

# WHEN TO PLANT

*'...go by the weather...'*

One year, on an unusually hot spring day, we planted a whole field of tomato plants. It was 30 °C (86 °F) that day, but two days later, to my horror, temperatures dropped dramatically and every single plant was killed by frost! That scenario, while tragic at the time, is rare, something that has happened to us only once in over 40 years of growing vegetables. I have always believed in planting early, and doing whatever I can to extend our growing season. Go by the weather rather than the calendar—if temperatures remain warm at the beginning of May, go ahead and put a few tomato plants into the garden rather than waiting another two or three weeks until the end of the month. Take a chance, live dangerously—you'll win with an earlier harvest far more times than you will lose plants to spring frosts. (For tips on protecting your plants from frost, see 'Extending the Growing Season' on page 35.)

*While I find this cartoon amusing, we have gained much more by planting early than we have ever lost.*

"LOOK HOW NICE EDMONTON'S SPRING WEATHER IS," *YOU SAID*..... "PLANT YOUR TOMATOES NOW," *YOU SAID!*.....

# BEFORE YOU PLANT, HARDEN-OFF

- 'Hardening-off' is a common term in the greenhouse industry. It simply means to gradually acclimatize plants from indoor to outdoor conditions, over a period of several days, before planting.

- The result of hardening-off is a tougher, hardier garden plant. Plants that have been hardened-off are usually sturdier, bushier and better able to withstand all types of weather than those which have not been hardened-off.

- Some greenhouses, but not all, harden-off plants before they sell them. When buying your plants, ask if this has been done. Often you can tell just by looking. Plants that have not been hardened-off are what growers call 'soft.' They are paler green, with longer, softer leaves and stems.

- If you raised your own tomato plants from seed without the benefit of a solarium or home greenhouse, you will need to gradually adjust the plants to the increased light levels outdoors. It's like sunbathing: if you sat in the bright sun all day on your first time out, you would get a sunburn. Well, plants can get sunburnt too. Choose a site with indirect or dappled sunlight that is also sheltered from the wind.

*This gardener took advantage of the space underneath his staked indeterminate tomato plants by growing celery, which can be transplanted into the garden at the same time as tomatoes in the spring.*

🌱 In my area, the peak growing season for tomatoes is from late May through August, when days are long and light levels are high. I take advantage of this by planting early.

- With most plants, exposure to cooler outdoor temperatures is all that is required for hardening-off. On early spring days when the temperature is between 15 and 18°C (59–64°F), set the pots of plants outdoors in a partially sunny site. Do not start them off in direct sunlight. Light levels outdoors are more than ten times as strong as indoors, and until the young plants have had time to adjust, too much light can burn them.

- If there is a risk of overnight frost, cover the pots with an old sheet, towel, blanket, piece of burlap or a cardboard box. You can bring them inside the house or into a heated garage, but be sure to move them outdoors again as soon as temperatures rise above freezing the next morning.

- As plants become hardened-off, you may find you need to water less. It's a good idea to keep soil moist but not wet; too much moisture results in plants staying 'soft.'

- Continue this gradual exposure for 7–10 days. At the end of this period, your plants will be ready to be transplanted into the garden.

# WHY PLANT EARLY?

- If frost were predicted one night in June or August, what would you do with your tomato plants? Protect them! Why not do the same thing in May?

- Far more young tomato plants are lost in spring to hot temperatures, wilting in dry soil, than to freezing-cold temperatures. Take a chance on earlier crops by putting a few of your plants into the garden around the date of the average last spring frost for your area—if the weather is good. Choose a sheltered location against a house wall or set hot caps (see page 36) over seedlings. Be prepared to cover plants if there is a risk of frost.

- By gambling on early planting, you usually win with a large yield of early, ripe tomatoes while your neighbours are still waiting for fruit to appear. If you lose, well, maybe you'll need to spend a few extra dollars on replacement plants—a small price to pay for the high chance of a greater yield. The odds of winning are good, better than you would get in Las Vegas.

## SEEDING

- Sow indoors about six weeks before transplanting. Refer to page 18 for details.

*Use protective coverings early in the season, when it is too cold for tomatoes to grow properly. Remove the coverings once the weather warms up; leaving protective coverings on too long results in stunted plants.*

## TRANSPLANTING

- Put the majority of your plants into the garden 1–2 weeks after the average last spring frost date for your area (see pages 37 and 38).

# EXTENDING THE GROWING SEASON

My growing season is short enough as it is, so I try to extend it rather than making it shorter. I believe that, in my area, July is the only month of the year in which there has never been a snowfall. Whenever temperatures fall to the freezing point, simply protect your plants overnight in any of the following ways.

- Here's a great tip for planting early—up to two weeks *before* the average last spring frost date for your area! Immediately after transplanting, put a tomato cage over each plant, and encircle it with plastic wrap, leaving the top open. This creates a mini-greenhouse around each plant, with the air inside several degrees warmer than outside. Each night at about 6:30 P.M., throw a towel over the entire cage, ensuring that the open top is completely covered. Your plants will be snug and warm inside this mini-greenhouse and will remain protected against cool overnight temperatures.

- If your tomato plants are growing in containers, move them indoors overnight.

- Cover tomato plants with burlap, an old towel, sheet, blanket, newspaper or a cardboard box—whatever is handy, except plastic sheeting, which has virtually no insulation value.

- Use plastic **hot caps**, which protect individual young plants by trapping warm air around the plants and insulating them against light frosts. You can buy hot caps or make your own by cutting the tops off large, clear plastic bottles and poking ventilation holes around the tops. Place these bottles upside-down overtop of young plants. As your plants mature, slit the hotcaps open to allow plants room to grow. Remove when plants grow tall enough to touch the top of the hot caps.

- Lay **row covers** over your plants. Row covers are made from lightweight, durable, spun-bonded polyester fabric and are available in various lengths and widths. When laid overtop of plants, they help to retain warmth, insulate the plants from wind and protect them against light frosts. Row covers also act as a barrier to insects. They are porous, allowing light, air and water to penetrate. Remove them once the danger of frost has passed.

- Not only do hot caps and row covers protect plants against cool temperatures and frost, they result in an earlier harvest. This is because the air around the plants is warmer and because you are able to plant up to a month earlier than usual. On a clear, sunny day, temperatures under a row cover will rise 6–9°C (43–48°F) above the outside air temperature. Young tomato plants stop growing at temperatures below 12°C (54°F).

Even a light frost will damage tomato plants. Frost-damaged plants may survive, but will be so set back in their growth that it is advisable to replace them with new plants. If you don't see new growth within a few days, I recommend buying new plants in order to ensure a harvest before frost arrives again in fall.

| City | Last Spring Frost | First Fall Frost | Frost-free Period (# of Days) | 37 |
|---|---|---|---|---|
| **Alberta** | | | | |
| Calgary | May 25 | September 15 | 112 | |
| Edmonton | May 6 | September 24 | 140 | |
| **British Columbia** | | | | |
| Vancouver | March 31 | November 3 | 216 | |
| Prince George | June 6 | August 31 | 85 | |
| **Manitoba** | | | | |
| Churchill | June 24 | September 9 | 76 | |
| Winnipeg | May 23 | September 22 | 121 | |
| **New Brunswick** | | | | |
| Fredericton | May 19 | September 23 | 126 | |
| **Newfoundland** | | | | |
| St. John's | June 1 | October 11 | 131 | |
| **Northwest Territories** | | | | |
| Yellowknife | May 27 | September 16 | 111 | |
| **Nova Scotia** | | | | |
| Halifax | April 30 | October 19 | 171 | |
| **Ontario** | | | | |
| Toronto | April 20 | October 29 | 191 | |
| **Prince Edward Island** | | | | |
| Charlottetown | May 16 | October 15 | 151 | |
| **Quebec** | | | | |
| Montreal | May 3 | October 8 | 157 | |
| **Saskatchewan** | | | | |
| Regina | May 24 | September 11 | 109 | |
| **Yukon** | | | | |
| Whitehorse | June 8 | August 30 | 82 | |
| **Alaska** | | | | |
| Anchorage | June 7 | August 23 | 75 | |
| **Colorado** | | | | |
| Denver | May 3 | October 8 | 157 | |
| **Idaho** | | | | |
| Boise | May 8 | October 9 | 153 | |
| **Illinois** | | | | |
| Chicago | April 14 | November 2 | 201 | |
| **Indiana** | | | | |
| Indianapolis | April 22 | October 20 | 179 | |
| **Louisiana** | | | | |
| New Orleans | February 20 | December 5 | 289 | |
| **Maine** | | | | |
| Portland | May 10 | September 30 | 142 | |

| City | Last Spring Frost | First Fall Frost | Frost-free Period (# of Days) |
|---|---|---|---|
| **Maryland** | | | |
| Baltimore | March 26 | November 13 | 230 |
| **Michigan** | | | |
| Detroit | April 28 | October 20 | 175 |
| **Montana** | | | |
| Helena | May 18 | September 18 | 123 |
| **New York** | | | |
| Buffalo | May 8 | October 11 | 155 |
| New York | April 11 | November 11 | 213 |
| **North Dakota** | | | |
| Bismarck | May 14 | September 20 | 129 |
| **Ohio** | | | |
| Cincinnati | April 14 | October 27 | 195 |
| **Oklahoma** | | | |
| Tulsa | March 30 | November 4 | 218 |
| **Oregon** | | | |
| Portland | April 3 | November 7 | 217 |
| **Tennessee** | | | |
| Knoxville | March 29 | November 6 | 222 |
| **Texas** | | | |
| San Antonio | March 3 | November 24 | 265 |
| **Vermont** | | | |
| Montpelier | May 18 | September 23 | 128 |
| **Virginia** | | | |
| Richmond | April 10 | October 26 | 198 |
| **Washington** | | | |
| Spokane | May 4 | October 5 | 153 |
| Seattle | March 24 | November 11 | 232 |
| **Wisconsin** | | | |
| Milwaukee | May 5 | October 9 | 150 |

The tomato is native to the Andes Mountains of South America. Wild tomato plants, ancestors of the cultivated varieties that we raise in our gardens, can still be found growing there today. Historians doubt that South American Indians grew or ate tomatoes before the Spanish conquest because there is no word for 'tomato' in their languages, and no illustrations of tomatoes on ancient artifacts.

## Tomato Marmalade

*A traditional recipe from my mother, Elsa Veregin, and a delicious change from citrus marmalade.*

12–16 ripe tomatoes
2 lemons
¼ cup (60 mL) cider
   vinegar
1 tbsp. (25 mL) finely
   chopped fresh ginger
3 cups (750 mL) sugar

Peel and coarsely chop tomatoes. Wash lemons, cut up and chop finely. Combine all ingredients in a large heavy saucepan. Bring to a boil over medium heat, reduce heat and simmer gently, leaving uncovered, until thick, about two hours. Ladle into hot, sterilized jars and seal. Makes about four 8-oz. (225 g) jars.

## Marinated Salad

For an easy and delicious marinated salad, layer slices of tomatoes and Spanish onions. Sprinkle with salt, pepper, a pinch of sugar and 1 tsp. (5 mL) **each** of minced fresh basil, olive oil and wine vinegar. Refrigerate for at least two hours before serving.

# HOW MANY TO PLANT

*'...better yields...'*

*Doris and Dave Grobel grow 40 tomato plants of six or seven different varieties. They have enough tomatoes for fresh eating from June to November, for canning about 40 quarts as well as plenty to give away.*

Years ago, few people bought less than a dozen tomato plants, but today this is the exception rather than the rule. Why is this so? Partly, I suppose, because most people no longer have space to grow that many tomato plants, nor do they have the time to look after them. Also, today's varieties have far higher yields. The variety Big Boy, for example, was received with great excitement for its remarkable yields when it was first introduced not long after World War II, but compared to newer varieties, its rating for yields has now declined to 'poor.'

Remember though, in any given year the same variety may not produce as well as it did in previous years, or it may produce even better. Fruit production is affected by factors beyond our control, such as weather, and by factors within our control, such as how well we look after our plants.

In 1987, Charles Wilber of Crane Hill, Alabama, harvested a total of 1,368 pounds (621 kg) of tomatoes from his four Better Boy plants, an average of 342 pounds (155 kg) per plant. The most tomatoes ever produced by a single plant was 16,897! This was recorded at the Tsukuba Science Expo Centre, Japan, on February 28, 1988, according to *The Guinness Book of Records*.

# A GENERAL RULE

- In general, I recommend six plants for a family of four: two plants for each adult and one for each child. That provides enough tomatoes for fresh sandwiches, salads and sauces.

- If the same family also wants to can or preserve their home-grown tomatoes, they should grow from 8 to 12 plants. Any more than this would feed much more than one family.

- The above is only a general rule, for people who eat a lot of tomatoes. Another family of four may only crave fresh tomatoes occasionally, and be satisfied with just one plant in a pot.

- A determinate tomato plant needs up to twice as much room as a staked, indeterminate plant. If you have limited space, the latter is probably a better choice. Don't forget though, if space is limited but you want lots of tomatoes, any tomato plant can be grown in a pot.

## DIFFERENCE IN YIELDS

The most exceptional yield I ever had was the year that we had just the right blend of sun and rain, resulting in literally thousands of ripe, juicy tomatoes—the field by our house looked red! There were so many tomatoes that we could not pick them all. One of our customers offered to fill his half-ton truck—if the price was right. Like a summertime Santa, he then drove home to his apartment building and presented

*Growing tomatoes is a family affair for Frank and Grace Timoteo. They grow several plants in their own garden, more in their son's and they exchange saved seed with a nephew in Toronto, Ontario.*

all the residents with more ripe tomatoes than they had ever dreamed of seeing.

*If you are grow-ing four tomato plants, why not grow an early, a mid-season and a late-maturing variety, along with a new vari-ety that you have never tried?*

- Remember that yields vary tremendously with seasonal conditions. In shadier gardens, plant more to compensate for lower yields.

- Generally, indeterminate plants have higher yields, but they require a little more work throughout the growing season.

*Although not the most decorative containers, black plastic pots absorb heat, warm the plant's roots and result in an earlier harvest of tomatoes.*

## My Favourite Tomato Is...

'If I were left with only one tomato variety, it would be Floramerica. Flavour is very high on my list of requirements.'

*H.A. Perkins, home gardener, Edmonton, Alberta*

'There are two tomato varieties that I think are outstanding. Centennial Rocket has good acidity and texture, and is my favourite tomato on pizza. Sweet Million is a very prolific cherry tomato that makes a great balcony plant and is expecially good in salads. Both are early-maturing, perfect for the Calgary climate.'

*Bryon Fischer, Horticulturist, Silver Springs Golf Course, Calgary, Alberta*

# TOMATO MANIA

**EVERY JUNE**, the population of Warren, Arkansas swells to three times its usual size, as between 15,000 and 20,000 people flock together for the Bradley County Pink Tomato Festival. Small girls compete in a pageant for the title of ' Little Miss Pink Tomato,' while adults wolf down all the tomatoes they can eat in a tomato-eating contest. This 40-year-old festival also has a tomato toss, a bobbing-for-tomatoes contest and an all-tomato luncheon.

**IN AUGUST**, it's time for the annual great Canadian Slice It Right Tomato Festival in Leamington, Ontario. This town's population triples during its festival, which attracts about 45,000 people. Festivities include a talent show for the title of 'Miss Tomato Festival,' a cooking-with-tomatoes contest, and the Tomato Stomp, in which teams compete to crush every tomato in sight with their bare feet!

**TOMATO FUDGE** anyone? If you want to try it, you'll have to attend the tomato festival at Reynoldsburg, Ohio, in early September. As well as carnival rides, a parade and a Tomato Queen, King, Little Prince and Little Princess, this 30-year-old festival includes a tomato food tent, with some pretty unusual creations, and free tomato juice for all. There are also 15 different ribbons for home-grown tomatoes, including prizes for the tallest tomato plant, and $100 per pound for the biggest tomato.

LIVINGSTON HOUSE PARK
Est. 1865

1202 GRAHAM ROAD

# TOMATOES, TOMATOES,

Many times I am asked which is my favourite tomato variety, and my answer always is that I have many tomato favourites. Every year I grow at least one and a half dozen varieties in my garden. I must have paste tomatoes for sauces, cherry tomatoes for salads and snacks, and larger tomatoes for sandwiches, soups and every other imaginable use. To ensure that I have fresh tomatoes for the longest period, I grow my favourite early variety, which ripens about mid-July, and my favourite small tomato, which ripens a couple of weeks earlier. I also grow a selection of my favourite later-maturing varieties, so that I have plants still bearing fruit when fall frosts arrive.

# TOMATOES...

A favourite is an extremely personal thing, and you will never find one group of people that entirely agrees with my choices. The 18 recommended varieties that follow are those that my family and the employees at our greenhouse have tested, tasted and determined to be the best performers overall. To make it easier for you to choose which ones you wish to grow, they are categorized by size—huge, extra-large, large, medium, small and cherry—and by use—paste, novelty and greenhouse.

These are my absolute favourite tomatoes...

# HUGE TOMATOES

*'...now that's how you grow tomatoes!'*

*For bigger tomatoes, pinch off a few flowers from each cluster.*

One of my favourite stories is about a gentleman who comes out to our greenhouses every spring to buy two dozen small tomato plants. He always also orders one large beefsteak-tomato plant, to be picked up later. When he returns in June, it is a colossal five-foot-tall (150 cm) specimen, with lots of full-sized tomatoes which are already turning red. This had always piqued my curiosity—why on earth would someone buy all those tomato plants and then be willing to pay us a premium for raising one more to mature size?

'Perhaps a gift for someone,' I thought and finally asked him. 'No,' he told me with a smile, 'it's not a gift. I take it home and pop it into my garden, when the neighbours aren't looking. The next time they lean over the fence, I show off my plant and say "Now that's how you grow tomatoes!" They think I grew it myself!'

'You know,' I said, ' the neighbours are going to catch on.' The man just laughed and said 'Well, the neighbours keep changing,' and off he went with his miraculous plant.

If you want to grow really big tomatoes, even without 'cheating,' stick to beefsteak varieties. Most gardeners know that 'beefsteak' means 'big,' but many are surprised to discover that is a *type* of tomato, rather than a specific variety. Beefsteak tomatoes are easily recognizable for their enormous size, and also for their distinctive, ridged and bumpy shape.

# RECOMMENDED VARIETIES

## BEEFMASTER

- Impressive yields of excellent beefsteak tomatoes; deep red, mouth-watering, full-flavoured; mostly 1 lb. (454 g), but occasionally 2 lbs. (908 g); strong, very vigorous vines; resistant to cracking and splitting.

- Indeterminate, hybrid; 80 days to maturity. Stake and prune.

### Other Comparable Varieties

*Bragger:* often described as a variety for gardeners who want to grow the biggest tomato on the block; low yields, but tomatoes grow up to 2 lbs. (908 g); slightly flattened shape; indeterminate, hybrid; 80 days to maturity.

*Brandywine*: a popular Amish heirloom variety; lower yields than newer varieties; dark pink, irregularly shaped tomatoes have exceptionally good, tangy flavour; average size 1–1 ½ lbs. (454–681 g); 'potato-leaf' foliage; indeterminate, open-pollinated; 80 days to maturity. (There is also a Yellow Brandywine with great-tasting, yellowish-orange fruit, but it needs 90–100 days to mature—too long for my area!)

If you want to save seed from your tomatoes, be sure it is an open-pollinated variety. You won't have good results with seed from hybrid plants. See 'Saving Seed' on page 132.

*Beefmaster tomatoes are solid, meaty, deep red and delicious.*

*Some gardeners take great pride in growing the biggest tomato on the block.*

Although colleagues in other areas of Canada rave about this variety, I've tried Brandywine twice and found the fruit never matured.

**Delicious**: an older variety that has been the world-record holder for size more than once, but most fruit weigh just over 1 lb. (454 g); best suited to warmer climates, blossoms drop when night temperatures are low; indeterminate, open-pollinated; 77 days to maturity.

**Oxheart**: an old-fashioned favourite with huge, pink, heart-shaped tomatoes up to 2 lbs. (908 g) with firm, solid, meaty flesh; good fresh, canned or juiced; large vines; indeterminate, open-pollinated; 80 days to maturity.

**Supersteak**: another 'super-size' tomato with fruit up to 2 lbs. (908 g); smoother fruit and less cat-facing than older beefsteaks; indeterminate, hybrid; 80 days to maturity.

**Ultra Boy**: higher yields make this the best of the 'Boy' series; average size over 1 lb. (454 g); smooth, globe-shaped tomatoes; indeterminate, hybrid; 72 days to maturity.

*Marie Desnoyers and Irene Rhodes love the heirloom variety Oxheart which was named for its fruit's supposed resemblance an ox's heart.*

*Beefsteak tomatoes are wonderful on pizza. Sprinkle uncooked pizza dough with mozzarella cheese and cover with thinly sliced beefsteak tomatoes. Sprinkle more mozzarella on top, add fresh basil or dried oregano and top with Parmesan cheese. Cook at 475°F (246°C) for 7–10 minutes or until dough is golden. Top with fresh tomato slices after cooking.*

Some gardeners wonder what to do with such huge tomatoes. I like stuffing them with other vegetables, rice or seafood, topped with bread crumbs or cheese. They make lovely serving containers, and they're great for sandwiches, because one slice covers an entire piece of bread. Huge tomatoes mean less work for cooking, canning and sauces.

**'You like to-ma-to and I like to-mah-to ...'**
- *Let's Call the Whole Thing Off,* George & Ira Gershwin, ©1937

And the true pronunciation is ... ? North Americans prefer to rhyme 'tomato' with 'potato,' but this may not have always been so. In *The Tomato in America,* Andrew F. Smith reports that a Colonial publication in South Carolina spelled the word 'tomawto,' suggesting that this was the original pronunciation.

# TIPS FOR GROWING HUGE TOMATOES

🍅🍅🍅 The world's largest tomato was the size of a human baby—a whopping 7 lb. 12 oz. (3.5 kg)! Gordon Graham of Edmond, Oklahoma, won himself a place in *The Guinness Book of Records* in 1986, with the variety Delicious.

Don't expect to break the world's record the first time you try! The people who grow the world's largest tomatoes have been at it for years. They keep charts, records and detailed notes, have elaborate growing methods and a few well-kept secrets. They often grow several different varieties and lots of plants, hoping to find that one titan of the tomato patch. There is no secret formula for guaranteed success, but I can certainly share a few tips that will set you on the right track.

- Choose a variety that is noted for the immense size of its fruit. Transplant as early as possible; the longer a tomato has to grow, the larger it will be. Use hot caps or other protectors to guard against cool spring temperatures.

- Consider planting your tomatoes in pots or raised beds, because the soil will warm faster than in open ground. It is also easier to improve soil quality, and you should have better drainage. The result of all this? Your plants should grow larger and faster.

- Give your plants lots of sun, and lots of room so they are not competing with neighbouring plants for nutrients, light or moisture.

- Your tomatoes will be larger if there are fewer of them. Some growers 'flower-prune,' decreasing each cluster from five blossoms to two. For the biggest tomatoes, limit each plant to just a few fruit.

- Water and fertilize religiously.

*Gardeners are proud of growing big tomatoes! Georgina Murray of Edmonton, Alberta, couldn't bear to give up her prize 3-lb. (1.2 kg) tomato, and so for the past seven years she has kept it in the freezer.*

- Prune off all suckers to allow more energy to be diverted to the fruit (see page 115).

- Tomatoes grown in home greenhouses are apt to be larger than garden-raised tomatoes, because a greenhouse environment is more easily controlled.

- Wish for sunshine! If the season is cooler and cloudier than normal, tomatoes will naturally be smaller.

The challenge of growing enormous tomatoes is particularly appealing to men. Many of our male customers are fussier than women in selecting plants, and like to boast more often about their results. Every year, at the end of the season, at least one man bursts into our greenhouses to show me 'the biggest tomato ever,' and I am always thrilled to see such success.

## Russian Borsch

*'A traditional Russian soup with a distinctively different taste from the usual borsch made with beets.'*

—Anne Norsten

⅓ cup butter
2 medium onions, diced
½ medium cabbage, shredded
4 large peeled tomatoes, chopped
4 large potatoes
1 tsp. salt
½ tsp. pepper
½ tsp. tartaric acid
3 tsp. dill seasoning (use fresh
   dill when available)

Melt butter in pot. Add onions. Cook on low heat for ½ hour. Stir. Add cabbage and cook until tender. Stir. Add chopped, peeled tomatoes. Boil potatoes in separate pot until soft, then mash in potato water. Add mashed potatoes and spices and simmer until ready to serve. Makes 8 generous portions.

# EXTRA-LARGE TOMATOES

*'...sweet and meaty...'*

So what's the difference between extra-large and huge tomatoes? Extra-large ones are slightly smaller, but there are more of them. When gardeners ask for the biggest tomato they can grow, I recommend the huge varieties. If they just want giant tomatoes, and lots of them, I recommend the extra-large varieties. Both are beefsteak types, a general term for old-fashioned, irregularly shaped, sweet and meaty tomatoes with large cores and few seeds. Originally, however, 'Beefsteak' was a Campbell's Soup Company brand-name for one large tomato in a single can.

Beefsteak tomatoes are so large and heavy that you may need to provide extra support to prevent branches from breaking.

# RECOMMENDED VARIETIES

## BIG BEEF

- One of the earliest-maturing beefsteaks; extra-heavy yields; meaty, flavourful fruit average 10–14 oz. (284–397 g); size remains extra-large even at the end of a long season; rounder and smoother than other beefsteak varieties; outstanding disease resistance.

- Indeterminate, hybrid; 73 days to maturity. Stake and prune.

- Not only is the grass greener on the other side of the fence, sometimes the tomatoes are better too! A friend told me that after his neighbour took a look at his Big Beef plants, which had produced great big, nicely shaped tomatoes despite a cool, cloudy summer, the neighbour became convinced that no other tomato would do, and has already ordered 50 Big Beef plants for next year.

- Big Beef was the 1994 winner of the All American Selections (AAS) award for overall superior performance. To be designated a winner, a

*Big Beef is a great-tasting hybrid variety.*

*Five-year-old Erik Grice proudly displays his Whopper.*

*Whopper produces clusters of full-flavoured tomatoes. It is a strong indeterminate variety best grown staked or in a cage.*

Any tomato plant, even the big beefsteaks, can be grown in a container. We often grow ours in 5-gallon (23-litre) buckets. Remember, bigger containers are better, and you will need to water less often.

new variety must prove to be greatly superior to existing varieties in flavour, yield, disease resistance and overall appearance. A panel of judges makes the final decision after receiving evaluations from various test gardens across North America.

*Big Beef, on the left, is smoother and rounder than most beefsteak varieties.*

- Big Beef scored top marks in *National Gardening* magazine's annual test of new vegetable varieties. In 1994, a record 93 per cent of test gardeners said they would grow Big Beef again.

*Ultra Sweet has an interior ripening gene which causes insides to turn pink while tomatoes are still green.*

- *The Tomato Club* newsletter publisher Bob Ambrose cites Big Beef as his favourite tomato. In the May/June 1995 issue of his newsletter, he explained why: 'It's big, beautiful, healthy and delicious, matures early and produces right to the onslaught of frost, with a stupendous harvest.' Ambrose said it took four Brandywine plants to equal the yield of a single Big Beef.

## WHOPPER

- Outyields by far most older beefsteak tomatoes and is earlier than most varieties that produce the same-size fruit; clusters of smooth, round tomatoes with great flavour; tomatoes average 14 oz. (397 g); resists cracking, blossom-end rot and most common tomato problems; a favourite of gardeners across North America.

- Indeterminate, hybrid; now 65 days to maturity. Stake and prune.

- If you can't find Whopper, it may be because this variety has been recently renamed 'OG50.' The new name is in honour of *Organic Gardening* magazine's 50th anniversary.

- The new Whopper or OG50 is even better! It is tastier, with better disease resistance, it matures earlier and resists cracking.

'Always peel tomatoes before using them in salads.'
Joyce Pearson, Home Service Director, Blue Flame Kitchen

*A single slice of Big Beef is large enough to cover a hamburger.*

## Other Comparable Varieties

**Better Boy**: one of North America's favourite home garden tomatoes; average fruit size 12–16 oz. (340–454 g); indeterminate, hybrid; 70 days to maturity.

**Big Boy**: one of the best-yielding new hybrids when it was introduced in 1949 but low yields compared to today's hybrids; average fruit size 10–16 oz. (284–454 g); indeterminate, hybrid; 78 days to maturity.

**Big Girl**: an effort to improve the older Big Boy variety, with more disease resistance and less cracking but prone to blossom-end rot; average fruit size 12 oz. (340 g); indeterminate, hybrid; 78 days to maturity.

**Ultra Sweet**: sweet, juicy and very flavourful, bright red tomatoes; average size 10 oz. (284 g); indeterminate, hybrid; 62 days to maturity.

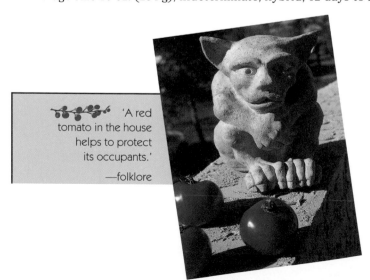

'A red tomato in the house helps to protect its occupants.'

—folklore

# Roast Beef (Jamaican-style)

*'Traditionally, roast beef is served with rice and peas\*, roast breadfruit, yams, sweet potatoes, avocado slices, fried plantains and so on. It is reserved for Sundays and festive occasions.'*

—Norma Benghiat, author, *Traditional Jamaican Cookery*

4 slices hot pepper, chopped
1 large tomato
2 cloves garlic, chopped
1 tablespoon salt
1 tablespoon black pepper
½ teaspoon thyme leaves
5 lb (2.25 kg) sirloin roast

⅓ cup (3 fl oz, 75 mL) oil
1 cup (8 fl oz, 250 mL) water
**Gravy**
2 large onions, sliced
2 tomatoes, chopped
1 clove garlic, chopped
3 slices hot pepper, chopped
salt

Mix together the first six ingredients. Make incisions all over the beef, and put a little of the mixture in each incision, leaving some to rub all over the roast. Tie it with string, place in a deep bowl, and leave for at least 2 hours, or preferably overnight in the refrigerator.

The beef can either be pot-roasted or cooked in the oven in the usual way. If it is to be pot-roasted, then heat the oil in a heavy iron pot or some other heavy braising pot. Remove the beef from the bowl and brown it all over, then add the water to the remains of the seasonings in the bowl and add this to the browned meat. Lower the heat, cover, and simmer until the meat is tender. This should take about 2 hours. Add the gravy ingredients and any vegetables you wish. Stir for a few minutes and taste for salt. If necessary, add a little water, bring back to simmering point, and serve.

If the meat is to be oven-roasted then transfer the meat from the bowl to a roasting pan. If you like the meat red inside, roast at 500°F, 260°C, gas 10 for about 30 minutes, until brown. If you like well done meat, roast at 400°F, 200°C, gas 6 for about an hour until brown. Remove the meat from the roasting pan and keep warm. Scrape all the drippings into a small saucepan over medium heat, and as soon as they start to sizzle, add the gravy ingredients. Stir for a minute or two, then add 2 cups (3/4 pint, 500 mL) of water and bring to the boil. Lower the heat slightly, and allow the gravy to reduce to the desired consistency, and add salt to taste. Enough for 8.

\* 'Rice and peas' is a Jamaican dish made with red kidney beans and rice.

# LARGE TOMATOES

*'...lots of nice, big tomatoes...'*

*Besides bragging rights, large tomato varieties are great for people who want lots of nice, big tomatoes for salads and sandwiches, for eating fresh or cooked, and for canning and sauces. Although the heavy-weight huge and extra-large tomatoes outweigh individual large tomatoes, overall the varieties in this category often out-yield the larger ones. I often recommend large tomato varieties for busy people, because they'll get high yields with less work, as many of these varieties are determinate and don't need pruning or staking.*

In the last 20 years, only four tomato varieties have been deemed worthy of an AAS award; Celebrity and Floramerica are two of them.

# RECOMMENDED VARIETIES

## CELEBRITY

- A wonderful variety for home gardeners; dependable and very productive under a wide range of growing conditions; highly rated for flavour; average size 8 oz. (227 g); outstanding disease resistance; resists cracking; 1984 AAS winner.

- Determinate, hybrid; 72 days to maturity. Use cage, no pruning.

- Celebrity was the first tomato to be named an AAS winner since Floramerica six years earlier. It was announced as the first determinate variety to be resistant to all the major tomato problems.

## CHAMPION

- A very popular variety bred especially for sandwiches—one slice covers a piece of bread; exceptionally high yield of solid, meaty tomatoes with just the right sweetness; size remains about 10 oz. (284 g) throughout the season; very adaptable, stocky plants set fruit even in hot weather; earlier harvests than many other varieties this size.

- Indeterminate, hybrid; 62 days to maturity. Stake and prune.

*Champion (left) can be relied on for consistent high yields of tasty tomatoes.*

*Celebrity (below) is early-maturing and has round, blemish-free tomatoes on wide-spreading plants.*

## FLORAMERICA

- The best bush beefsteak tomato—most other beefsteak tomatoes are indeterminate; solid, deep red tomatoes average 8-10 oz. (227–284 g); flavour is wonderful fresh, canned or juiced; 1978 AAS winner; outstanding disease resistance; excellent for canning; my number one recommendation for farm women.

- Determinate, hybrid; 75 days to maturity. Use cage, no pruning.

- Floramerica performs well in almost any weather, from Florida to Canada, and has inbred resistance to over 15 diseases and tomato problems.

- These are wide-spreading plants that need more room than most other varieties.

*Floramerica is an award-winning variety that produces plenty of good, meaty tomatoes for canning, enough to keep you well stocked through winter.*

## NORTHERN EXPOSURE

- An exciting new variety bred especially for areas with short summers and cooler temperatures, but also undeterred by early-summer heat waves; great-tasting, firm, smooth tomatoes with very few seeds and consistent nice shape; average weight about 8 oz. (227 g).

- Determinate, hybrid; 67 days to maturity. Use cage, no pruning.

*Northern Exposure has the mouth-watering flavour and aroma of a beefsteak-type tomato, with very few seeds.*

- Unlike other tomatoes, Northern Exposure has the ability to set a heavy crop of fruit early in the season, regardless of persistent cool weather. Low temperatures when tomato plants are pollinating often result in misshapen fruit. Northern Exposure tomatoes are consistently perfectly shaped, indicating a superior ability to pollinate well during cool temperatures.

*In their first attempt at growing tomatoes, the Stang sisters Jaclyn, 5, and Katelyn, 4, competed to see who could do best.*

- Northern Exposure was by far the most popular tomato at our green-houses in 1995. It also, however, has the dubious distinction of being the most commonly misnamed by gardeners who know what they want but cannot quite recall if it's Southern Exposure, Northern Alberta, Northern Tomato ....

- Don't get confused by this variety's name! One gardener asked me if he could still grow it, even though his vegetable garden did not have a northern exposure. Like any other tomato, Northern Exposure likes lots of sun. Gardens with southern exposures are ideal.

*A single Northern Exposure tomato is enough for three to four sandwiches. The plants are fairly compact and suited to growing in large containers.*

*The classic BLT is a favourite way to enjoy fresh tomatoes.*

## SUPER FANTASTIC

- The highest-yielding beefsteak variety; very meaty, delicious, 9–10 oz. (255–284 g), rounder and smoother than many beefsteaks; gardeners who grow it say this is one of the best tomatoes available; grows well in both gardens and greenhouses.

- Indeterminate, hybrid; 70 days to maturity. Stake and prune.

*Super Fantastic is popular for its abundance of delicious, juicy tomatoes and great performance in gardens across the country.*

- Super Fantastic is one of the best-selling tomatoes at our greenhouses, and one that I have grown in my garden for years. When we first picked up this variety, Super Fantastic was on the leading edge of breeding technology, with extremely high yields, built-in disease resistance and an ability to set fruit at a wide range of temperatures. It was introduced as an improvement on Fantastic, once one of the most widely grown tomatoes in North America.

## Other Comparable Varieties

***Bush Beefsteak:*** an old standard with good yields of early-maturing, meaty tomatoes; average size 8 oz. (227 g); common in Canada and northern U.S.; determinate, open-pollinated; 62 days to maturity.

***Crimson Fancy:*** excellent for first-time gardeners, good results for minimum care; sweet, round, 8-oz. (227 g) tomatoes; determinate, hybrid; 75 days to maturity.

***President:*** developed for home gardeners; meaty, 8-oz. (227 g) tomatoes with good flavour; great disease resistance; determinate, hybrid; 68 days to maturity.

**Starfire**: an older Canadian variety that grows best in sandy soils; 8-oz. (227 g) tomatoes; determinate, open-pollinated; 56 days to maturity.

**Superbush**: another variety bred for little care; vigorous, upright plants need no pruning, staking or caging; meaty, 8-oz. (227 g) fruit; great for containers; determinate, hybrid; 70 days to maturity.

**Terrific**: a home-garden hybrid noted for its excellent taste and ability to set fruit in hot weather; best for southern gardeners; average size 8–10 oz. (227–284 g); indeterminate, hybrid; 70 days to maturity.

**Ultra Girl**: firm, bright red tomatoes with good flavour; average fruit size 7–9 oz. (198–255 g); crack-resistant; determinate, hybrid; 62 days to maturity.

*John Gabriel displays the impressive yield from Super Fantastic.*

All-America Selections (AAS) awards indicate that a new variety has proven to be greatly superior to existing varieties in flavour, yield, disease resistance and overall appearance. A panel of judges makes the final decision after receiving evaluations from various test gardens across North America. This award distinguishes only superior varieties and not the best new ones for any given year. AAS is an educational, non-profit organization that has been evaluating seed-grown flowers and vegetables since 1933. There are no vegetable winners for 1996.

In over 60 years, only 16 tomato varieties have been selected for this award. Previous award-winners that are still available include:

| | | |
|---|---|---|
| Big Beef | 1994 | (Petoseed) |
| Husky Gold | 1993 | (Petoseed) |
| Celebrity | 1984 | (Petoseed) |
| Floramerica | 1978 | (University of Florida) |
| Small Fry | 1970 | (Petoseed) |

*Darcy Leiter (left) and Jim Nau (right) of Ball Seed gave my son Bill a tour of their trial gardens at Chicago, Illinois.*

# MEDIUM-SIZED TOMATOES

*'…. first of the season…'*

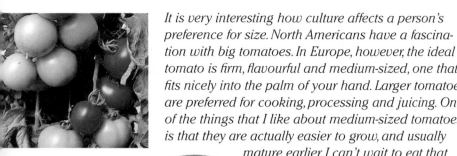

It is very interesting how culture affects a person's preference for size. North Americans have a fascination with big tomatoes. In Europe, however, the ideal tomato is firm, flavourful and medium-sized, one that fits nicely into the palm of your hand. Larger tomatoes are preferred for cooking, processing and juicing. One of the things that I like about medium-sized tomatoes is that they are actually easier to grow, and usually mature earlier. I can't wait to eat that first lovely fresh tomato. To me, there's nothing nicer than a fresh tomato sandwich made from garden tomatoes— especially the first one of the season!

# RECOMMENDED RED VARIETIES

## COUNTER

- An exceptional variety with heavy yields of perfect, round tomatoes; tangy flavour; tomatoes average 3–5 oz. (85–142 g); great resistance to blossom-end rot; open growth habit makes vines easy to work with; extremely popular in Europe; a greenhouse type that is also excellent in open gardens.

- Indeterminate, hybrid; 60 days to maturity. Stake and prune.

- One year I planted all of our tomatoes at the north end of our vegetable garden, beside a long row of large poplars. I never even thought about those trees' long, wide-spreading, thirsty roots! Because of that, no matter how much water I gave our tomato plants, it was never enough—the trees used it all. As a result, I had serious problems with blossom-end rot on all of our tomatoes—except Counter! What appeared to be a terrible mistake yielded me some invaluable information.

*Heartland grows only 3–4 feet (90–120 cm) tall and looks like a lovely little tree, making it ideal for containers and small gardens. It performs well with high yields in gardens across the country.*

My daughter-in-law Valerie rates Counter as her favourite tomato because of the firmness of its ripe fruit and its wonderful tangy flavour.

*Lucy Krisco likes Counter for its long trusses of perfect, round tomatoes.*

## HEARTLAND

- One of the best varieties for growing in containers; wonderful flavour; average fruit size 6–8 oz. (170–227 g); attractive, stocky, compact plants with large leaves that provide good protection from sun-scald.

- Semi-determinate, hybrid; 68 days to maturity. Stake or cage; do not prune.

- I call Heartland 'The Condo Tomato' because these compact plants are perfect for growing in containers on condominium balconies or patios, but are also pretty enough to be grown right in the middle of a flowerbed. Whenever I see an apartment building with flowerbeds lining the entrance walkway, I can hardly resist ringing the manager's buzzer to suggest he or she plant a couple of Heartlands in those beds. Wouldn't it be nice if the apartment residents could pick fresh, ripe tomatoes as they came home from work!

## Other Comparable Varieties

**Bounty**: one of the original varieties we grew at our greenhouses; good yields with little care required; tomatoes average 6–8 oz. (170–227 g); determinate, open-pollinated; 64 days to maturity.

**Husky Red**: plants similar to Heartland; fruit average 5–7 oz. (142–198 g); good in containers; semi-determinate, hybrid; 70 days to maturity.

**Jet Star**: an excellent-tasting variety with 8-oz. (227 g) fruit; indeterminate, hybrid; 72 days to maturity.

**Moneymaker**: a popular variety, especially in England; reliable producer in cooler regions; high temperatures cause problems with fruit set; average size 5–6 oz. (142–170 g); indeterminate, open-pollinated; 70 days to maturity.

**Rutgers**: one of the best-known older tomato varieties, originally developed by Campbell's Soup Company in 1928 but not widely grown until the 1940s; average fruit size 7–8 oz. (198–227 g); indeterminate, open-pollinated; 85 days to maturity.

**Springset**: high-yielder that produces most of its crop within a few days; reliable producer but subject to sun-scald; tomatoes average 5 oz. (142 g); determinate, hybrid; 65 days to maturity.

Seed for hybrid varieties, especially specialized or imported varieties, is more expensive than standard (open-pollinated) tomato seed, because of the work involved in breeding and production. I am willing to pay a slight premium because, as with everything else, you get what you pay for.

# RECOMMENDED EARLY VARIETIES

## EARLY GIRL

- The earliest-maturing slicing tomato and one of my all-time favourite varieties; large clusters of great-tasting, rich red, meaty tomatoes, very flavourful; average size 5 oz. (142 g); produces over a long period; very dependable; sturdy vines with good foliage protection against sun-scald; the improved version has better disease resistance than the original Early Girl.

- Indeterminate, hybrid; 52 days to maturity. Stake and prune.

- Our greenhouse manager Dave Grice says he has yet to hear of a customer who was disappointed with Early Girl. In fact, many customers grow nothing but this variety. We have sold more Early Girl tomatoes in the last ten years than any other variety.

*I always say that everyone who grows tomatoes should have at least one Early Girl in the yard. This variety ripens earlier than most, giving you a head start on harvesting ripe tomatoes.*

In my view, the only thing early about some varieties is their names. I consider any tomato that takes longer than 60 days to be mid-season, and any over 70 days to be late-maturing.

*Early Girl is the earliest-maturing slicing tomato.*

 Most tomato seedlings look the same, but Heartland has such a distinctive, stocky growth habit that even the seedlings are instantly recognizable.

## Other Comparable Early Varieties

*Earliana*: a favourite early in the century, but being taken over by newer varieties with better yields and disease resistance; mellow-flavoured tomatoes average 4–5 oz. (113–142 g); indeterminate, open-pollinated; 62 days to maturity.

*Early Cascade*: good-tasting with high yields of juicy tomatoes in clusters produced into the fall; average fruit size 5–6 oz. (142–170 g); indeterminate, hybrid; 55 days to maturity.

*Early Pick*: sets fruit well in areas with low night temperatures; tomatoes average 4–5 oz. (113–142 g); determinate, hybrid; 62 days to maturity.

*Fireball*: bred for gardeners with short growing seasons; produces a heavy crop for a few days and then is spent; average fruit size 4–5 oz. (113–142 g); determinate, open-pollinated; 60 days to maturity.

*Manitoba*: an older, early-maturing Canadian variety now being taken over by newer and better-tasting varieties; tomatoes average 6 ½ oz. (185 g); determinate, open-pollinated; 60 days to maturity.

*Oregon Spring*: developed by Oregon State University for short-season gardeners; good yields of  tomatoes averaging 4–7 oz. (113–198 g); few seeds; determinate, open-pollinated; 58 days to maturity.

*Scotia*: sets fruit well in cool temperatures; red tomatoes with green shoulders; average size 4 oz. (113 g); determinate, open-pollinated; 60 days to maturity.

 'Almost everyone who tasted Lemon Boy last year liked the flavour.'
*Dave Matthews, gardening columnist, Calgary, Alberta*

# RECOMMENDED YELLOW VARIETIES

*Yellow tomatoes are noted for their mild flavour. Lemon Boy is more flavourful and has a nicer colour than most yellow varieties.*

## LEMON BOY

- Unusual, clear lemon-yellow colour inside and out; more attractive than golden types; smooth, shapely tomatoes with sweet, mild flavour; average fruit size 7 oz. (198 g); very productive.

- Indeterminate, hybrid; 72 days to maturity. Stake and prune.

- Lemon Boy's flavour is far better than what many people would expect from a yellow tomato. I think more gardeners should try this variety.

🌿 It is commonly believed that yellow tomatoes are low-acid, but tests have shown that their acidity levels are actually the same as red tomatoes.

🌿 Over 12 million tomato seeds were sent into orbit inside a satellite in 1984, and six years later the space shuttle Columbia brought them home. NASA then distributed the seeds to teachers across North America to grow in classrooms.

*A mixed salad with Lemon Boy tomatoes is one of my daughter-in-law's favourite ways to serve fresh vegetables.*

## Other Comparable Yellow Varieties

**Golden Boy**: golden-orange tomatoes; average 4–6 oz. (113–170 g); matures a bit late for our region; indeterminate, hybrid; 80 days to maturity.

**Husky Gold**: bushy, stocky plants similar to Heartland; tomatoes average 5–7 oz. (142–198 g); 1993 AAS winner; semi-determinate, hybrid; 70 days to maturity.

**Taxi**: heavy yields of bright yellow, sweet, juicy tomatoes; average size 4–6 oz. (113–170 g); determinate, open-pollinated; 70 days to maturity.

### Metric Conversions

Multiply **ounces** by 30 to get **millilitres**
Multiply **millilitres** by 0.034 to get **ounces**

Multiply **cups** by 0.24 to get **litres**
Multiply **litres** by 4.2 to get **cups**

Multiply **pints** by 0.47 to get **litres**
Multiply **litres** by 2.1 to get **pints**

Multiply **quarts** by 0.95 to get **litres**
Multiply **litres** by 1.06 to get **quarts**

Multiply **gallons** by 3.8 to get **litres**
Multiply **litres** by 0.26 to get **gallons**

Multiply **ounces** by 28 to get **grams**
Multiply **grams** by 0.035 to get **ounces**

Multiply **pounds** by 0.45 to get **kilograms**
Multiply **kilograms** by 2.2 to get **pounds**

1 tsp. = 5 ml
1 tbsp. = 15 ml
1 oz. = 30 ml
4 oz. = 120 ml
1 cup (8 oz.) = 240 ml

# Mild Salsa

*'A great way to preserve a bumper crop of tomatoes.'*

—Patti Shenfield, author, *Flavors of Home:*
*Creative Cooking from Down-Home to Gourmet*

| | |
|---|---|
| 15 lbs. (6.5 kg) | tomatoes, peeled and chopped (20 cups / 5 litres) |
| 5 | fresh jalapeño peppers (save seeds from 2) |
| 8–10 cups (2–2.5 litres) | chopped onions |
| 2 | large sweet green peppers, finely chopped |
| 2 cups (500 ml) | vinegar |
| 13 oz. (369 ml) | tomato paste |
| 1 tbsp. (15 ml) | pickling salt |
| 1 | garlic clove, minced |
| ½ cup (125 ml) | sugar |
| 1 tsp. (5 ml) | black pepper |
| ¼ tsp.(1 ml) | cumin |
| 1 tsp. (5 ml) | chili powder |
| ¼ tsp. (1 ml) | cayenne |
| ¾ cup (175 ml) | cold water |
| ½ cup (125 ml) | cornstarch |

Prepare 14 pint (2-cup / 500 ml) jars. Place whole tomatoes in boiling water for 30 seconds or until skins split. Remove tomatoes with a slotted spoon and place in ice-cold water. Slip off skins. Core and dice tomatoes and place in a very large kettle. Using gloves, dice jalapeño peppers. Save seeds from 2 peppers and add to the pot with the peppers. Add all remaining ingredients except water and cornstarch. Bring to a boil and simmer until vegetables are tender, about 10–15 minutes. Dissolve cornstarch in cold water and stir into hot salsa. Simmer for 5 more minutes. Ladle into hot sterilized jars. Process in a boiling water bath for 15 minutes. Serve with nachos or your favourite Mexican dishes. This is also great over scrambled eggs or on hot dogs.

**Yield:** 14 pints—14, 2-cup (500 ml) jars.
**Note:** You can purée half of the tomatoes for a less chunky salsa. If you want a hotter salsa, add more jalapeño peppers or pass the Tabasco when you open the jar. This can be used immediately. Wear gloves when chopping hot peppers, or use a blender or food-processor, to avoid transferring the 'heat' to your hands (it doesn't wash off with soap and water, and can irritate or burn sensitive skin).

# SMALL TOMATOES

*'...twice the size of a cherry tomato...'*

*Tumbler matures weeks earlier than most tomato varieties.*

Often, small tomatoes are listed with cherry tomato varieties but I believe there is enough of a size difference that small tomatoes deserve their own category. Small tomatoes are generally twice the size of the average cherry tomato. A variety that was introduced in the last few years is so outstanding that it has become the only small tomato we recommend. Tumbler was bred especially for hanging baskets. I hang a basket of tomatoes above my deck, in place of flowers. My friends always comment on what a great idea this is, while they are picking and eating the ripe fruit.

# RECOMMENDED VARIETIES

## TUMBLER

- The heaviest yields of any tomato relative to plant size; impressive abundance of small, tasty tomatoes; average size 2 inches (5 cm) round; excellent in hanging baskets and containers; branches cascade over sides of containers; use cage if planted in garden.

- Determinate, hybrid; 49 days to maturity. No pruning or support required.

- Because of its unique growth habit, Tumbler is best suited to growing in containers. Use large containers or you will find yourself unable to keep up with watering demands. I recommend a minimum size of 12 inches (30 cm) for hanging baskets and other pots.

- This variety produces so many tomatoes that it needs lots of fertilizer and water. I fertilize Tumbler plants two times a week—twice as often as usual—and water every day.

- Keep Tumbler's trailing branches off the ground, safe from slugs and protected from contact with soil or concrete, which can lead to rot or disease. Choose tall containers, a pedestal-type planter, or set the pots on top of a stool.

- If there is a risk of frost, protect plants in hanging baskets from frost by bringing them indoors overnight.

Commercial growers start seeding earlier than home gardeners, because greenhouse conditions are ideal for raising plants. Seedlings that have grown too long inside your home usually become weak and stretched before you can transplant them outdoors.

*A single Tumbler plant produces up to 6 pounds (2.7 kg) of sweet, bright red tomatoes.*

## Other Comparable Varieties

**Basket King:** another variety bred especially for containers; grown for its appearance as much as for its thin-skinned, sweet tomatoes; average fruit size 1 ¾ inches (4.5 cm); determinate, hybrid; 55 days to maturity.

**Centennial Rocket:** (also known as Rocket) the one we used to grow, before Early Girl was developed (see page 66); tomatoes average 3–4 oz. (85–113 g); small vines suitable for containers; developed for areas with short growing seasons; often listed in seed catalogues under the heading 'Early'; determinate, open-pollinated; 52 days to maturity.

**Patio:** stocky plants about 2 ½ feet (75 cm) tall; average fruit size 3–4 oz. (85–113 g) and 2 inches (5 cm) across; good for containers; determinate, hybrid; 70 days to maturity.

**Swift:** small, flavourful tomatoes on bushy plants that don't need support; dependable fruit-set at lower temperatures; average fruit size 2 inches (5 cm); determinate, open-pollinated; 54 days to maturity.

**Sub-Arctic:** an early-maturing variety bred for northern areas where tomatoes won't normally grow; we used to grow this variety but replaced it with Early Girl (see page 66), which is larger and tastier; average size 2 oz. (57 g); determinate, open-pollinated; 48 days to maturity.

*Tumbler was developed to grow in hanging baskets.*

## My Favourite Tomato Is...

'Tumbler is an excellent variety with trailing foliage and a mass of sweet-flavoured, bright red fruit. I like to mix Tumbler with other bedding plants in containers or hanging baskets for a colourful, fruitful display on the patio. I also love the sweet flavour of Gardener's Delight, a very popular variety in the U.K. for the greenhouse or outdoors, with long trusses of small cherry tomatoes.'

—*Brian Smith, owner of Woodlea Nurseries, Hampshire, England, and past chairman of the British Bedding and Pot Plant Association*

*Seed for Tumbler is expensive, but its high yields make it worth the price. It takes three plants of comparable varieties to produce as many tomatoes as a single Tumbler!*

'At one time I counted over 100 tomatoes on my Tumbler and it is still producing!'—*comment from my friend Joan Rossall, Edmonton, Alberta, during a cool, cloudy summer (not the best conditions for tomato production).*

---

Here are the meanings behind some commonly used tomato acronyms:

**AAS** All-America Selections winner; AAS is an educational, non-profit organization that evaluates new flower and vegetable varieties and issues awards to those that are outstanding.

**DTM** days to maturity; the length of time from transplanting to harvest.

**F1** means the variety is hybrid; 'F1' indicates the first filial generation, or first offspring (you won't have good results if you save plant seed from hybrid tomatoes).

**ISN** interdeterminate short-node; a term sometimes used to describe semi-determinate tomato plants.

**OP** open-pollinated; pollinated naturally by wind or insects, without human intervention (you *can* save the seeds of plants you've grown from this seed and plant it again).

**St** stemphylium (grey leaf spot), a fungus that causes brownish-grey dead spots on foliage.

**TMV** tobacco mosaic virus; a viral disease that can affect tomatoes.

**VFNT** indicates resistance to the tomato diseases verticillium, fusarium, tobacco mosaic virus and nematodes (nematodes are actually extremely tiny, worm-like organisms, but symptoms in affected plants are similar to those caused by diseases, so they are usually listed together).

# CHERRY TOMATOES

*'...that extra sweetness...'*

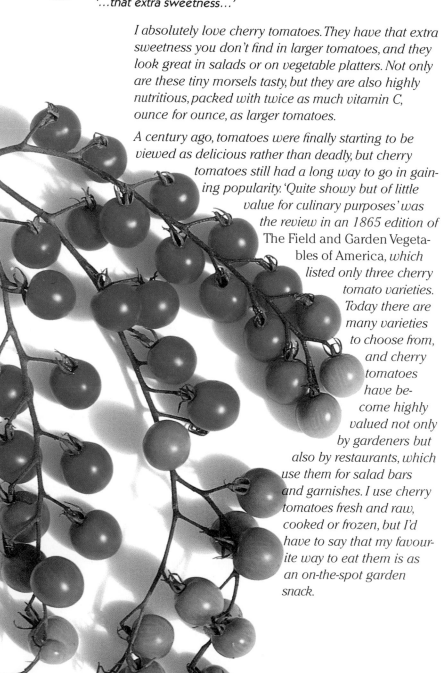

I absolutely love cherry tomatoes. They have that extra sweetness you don't find in larger tomatoes, and they look great in salads or on vegetable platters. Not only are these tiny morsels tasty, but they are also highly nutritious, packed with twice as much vitamin C, ounce for ounce, as larger tomatoes.

A century ago, tomatoes were finally starting to be viewed as delicious rather than deadly, but cherry tomatoes still had a long way to go in gaining popularity. 'Quite showy but of little value for culinary purposes' was the review in an 1865 edition of The Field and Garden Vegetables of America, *which listed only three cherry tomato varieties. Today there are many varieties to choose from, and cherry tomatoes have become highly valued not only by gardeners but also by restaurants, which use them for salad bars and garnishes. I use cherry tomatoes fresh and raw, cooked or frozen, but I'd have to say that my favourite way to eat them is as an on-the-spot garden snack.*

*I eat Sungold cherry tomatoes like candy, and I actually serve them up that way too. At a recent dinner party, my guests emptied a glass candy-dish filled with Sungold tomatoes as quickly as I could fill it.*

*Sungold continues to produce an abundance of beautiful, golden tomatoes well into fall. They keep their superb flavour even if not picked immediately.*

# RECOMMENDED VARIETIES

## SUNGOLD

- One of the world's best-tasting tomatoes; very sweet, thin-skinned, golden, 1-inch (2.5 cm) cherry tomatoes; extremely vigorous plants with long, spreading branches.

- Indeterminate, hybrid; 60 days to maturity. Stake and prune.

- Sungold tomatoes taste so good that very few of them make it into my kitchen! I eat most of these delicious cherry tomatoes right off the vine.

- If you find you are having problems with the fruit cracking, pick these tomatoes as soon as they turn from green to gold, rather than waiting for a brighter orange colour.

Sungold tomatoes are very sweet, thin-skinned and even more nutritious than the average vine-ripened tomato! Orange tomatoes have the highest vitamin A content.

When using cherry tomatoes in baked casseroles or rice and vegetarian dishes, cut them in half and add them to the pot just after removing it from the oven. Stir to barely cover the cut halves, replace the lid and let stand for a moment or two. There will be enough heat from the cooked dish to heat the cherry tomatoes but not enough to adversely affect their texture.

## SWEET 100

- One of the highest-yielding and most popular cherry tomatoes; hundreds of cherry tomatoes over a long period of harvest; extremely sweet, tangy, 1-inch (2.5 cm) fruit hang in clusters on long branches, like bunches of grapes; very ornamental plants grow 10 feet (3 m) or taller; superb in large containers.

- Indeterminate, hybrid; 60 days to maturity. Stake and prune.

- Sweet 100 has undoubtedly been the most popular cherry tomato among home gardeners for the past 20 years, and it remains one of my favourite varieties today. It adapts easily to climates as varied as those from Canada to the southern U.S.A.

- Supersweet 100 has improved disease resistance and greater tolerance to cracking, but I still prefer the original Sweet 100. In my garden, Sweet 100 outperformed Supersweet 100 and Sweet Million for yields, quality of fruit and overall growth.

## TINY TIM

- Dwarf ornamental cherry variety ideal for children, great in patio pots or windowsill gardens; produces lots of round, bright red, ¾-inch (2 cm) cherry tomatoes; great flavour; neat plants just 18 inches (45 cm) tall; needs minimal care.

*Sweet 100 bears its fruit in long trusses, a bit like grapes, producing a very decorative effect on the plant.*

*Tiny Tim is an ideal variety for children because the plants have a good success rate for producing ripe tomatoes, even when cared for by eager but inexperienced young gardeners. These plants are a little more forgiving than most tomatoes, and rarely crack or split on the vine or while being picked.*

- Determinate, open-pollinated; 45 days to maturity. No support or pruning required.

- Because of its dwarf size, Tiny Tim is one of the few tomato varieties that can be grown in a small pot. I often grow this variety in windowboxes with flowers.

## Other Comparable Varieties

*Better Bush Cherry Gold*: golden cherry tomatoes on an attractive, bushy plant; average size 1–1 ½ inches (2.5–3.5 cm); good for containers or garden; disease-resistant; semi-determinate, hybrid; 70 days to maturity.

*Gardener's Delight*. good yields of extra-sweet, tangy, bright red cherry tomatoes in clusters of 6–12; average fruit size 1–1 ½ inches (2.5–3.5 cm); large plants; a parent of Sweet 100; indeterminate, open-pollinated; 65 days to maturity.

The tallest recorded tomato plant was a Sweet 100 that grew to 53 ½ feet (16.3 m): 28 feet (8.5 m) up one side of a scaffold and 25 feet (7.6 m) up the other. Had it been upright, this cherry tomato plant would have been taller than the average tree!

*Warren Bailey's Sweet 100 plant (left) grew to an impressive size.*

*Sungold (below) is a wild-looking plant with enough tangy-sweet tomatoes to share with family, friends, neighbours, the mail carrier....*

Don't forget that cherry tomatoes can be enjoyed year-round! After washing them, I often can them whole with skins on, or freeze them intact without blanching, placed inside a plastic freezer bag. When these cherry tomatoes are cooked, the skins will slip off and float to the top of soups or sauces, where they are easily removed.

**Husky Cherry Gold**: good yields of vibrant gold cherry tomatoes; excellent flavour; sturdy, compact plants; semi-determinate, hybrid; 72 days to maturity.

**Husky Cherry Red**: similar to above but red and matures slightly earlier; semi-determinate, hybrid; 68 days to maturity.

**Sweet Chelsea**: high yields of sweet cherry tomatoes; average size 1–1 ½ inches (2.5–3.5 cm); disease- and crack-resistant variety; indeterminate, hybrid; 64 days to maturity.

**Sweet Gold**: a version of Sweet Million with golden cherry tomatoes; indeterminate, hybrid; 60 days to maturity.

**Sweet Million**: very sweet, tangy cherry tomatoes; average size 1 inch (2.5 cm); disease- and crack-resistant; large plants; indeterminate, hybrid; 65 days to maturity.

**Supersweet 100**: a variety developed from Sweet 100 with improved disease resistance; very sweet cherry tomatoes slightly larger than Sweet 100; indeterminate, hybrid; 65 days to maturity.

**Yellow Cherry**: huge harvest of bright yellow, $^3/_4$-inch (2 cm) cherry tomatoes; makes a colourful addition to salads; vigorous plants; indeterminate, open-pollinated; 70 days to maturity.

*Vi Lumsden likes Sweet 100 for its multitude of early, sweet cherry tomatoes.*

*His own home-grown cherry tomatoes are one of the few vegetables that 7-year-old Morgan Fallis loves to eat.*

To encourage the love of gardening, Hole's Greenhouses gives away hundreds of Tiny Tim tomato plants to children every spring.

**81**

## Varieties Comparable to Tiny Tim

***Cherry Gold:*** a version of Tiny Tim with yellow cherry tomatoes; very compact plants good for pots and windowboxes; determinate, open-pollinated; 45 days to maturity.

***Red Robin:*** a later-maturing, miniature version only 6 inches (15 cm) tall; tart flavour; determinate, hybrid; 55 days to maturity.

***Small Fry:*** 1-inch (2.5 cm) red cherry tomatoes; plants shorter and mature later than Tiny Tim; good in hanging baskets because of its spreading growth; adaptable to adverse conditions; 1970 AAS winner; determinate, hybrid; 72 days to maturity.

***Toy Boy:*** plants are slightly shorter and fruit slightly larger than Tiny Tim, but matures later; plants are 14 inches (36 cm) tall and suitable for hanging baskets; determinate, hybrid; 68 days to maturity.

***Yellow Canary:*** tiny plants just 6–8 inches (15–20 cm) tall with 1-inch (2.5 cm), yellow cherry tomatoes; handles lower light levels fairly well; determinate, hybrid; 55 days to maturity.

Currant tomatoes (*Lycopersicon pimpinella*) are even smaller than cherry tomatoes, closer in size to blueberries. These tiny, firm, tart tomatoes are all the rage in many gourmet restaurants, but many gardeners consider the fruit too small to be worth the bother of growing.

*Whether or not marigolds really do repel insects, these flowers make a great companion to tomatoes for looks alone.*

# GROWING TIPS FOR CHERRY TOMATOES

- All cherry tomatoes are marvellous in containers. Be sure to use large containers for large plants or you will find yourself unable to keep up with watering demands.

- Combine dwarf varieties like Tiny Tim with herbs and flowers in flowerbeds, mixed planters or windowboxes.

- Varieties that are extremely vigorous with long, branching vines and an abundance of fruit, such as Sungold and Sweet 100, should be trained to keep them from becoming unruly. When staked in a pot on your backyard deck, this type of cherry tomato will take up no more room than a very large-fruited tomato variety.

- One gardener I know chose to leave Sungold unstaked, and simply set her pot on top of a 3-foot-high (90 cm) outdoor table and let the unstaked branches trail down. With that added height, the fruit was kept off the ground, safe from marauding slugs and protected from contact with soil or concrete, which can lead to rotting fruit.

*Vine-ripened, garden-grown cherry tomatoes taste far better than those found at grocery stores or restaurant salad bars. The reason for this is that the leading commercial cherry tomato variety was bred to ship well and look pretty rather than to taste great.*

- Be very diligent with fertilizing and watering because such active growth demands a lot of nutrients and moisture. Feed with 20-20-20 fertilizer once a week, and be prepared to water almost every day. You'll be rewarded with more cherry tomatoes than you can possibly eat by yourself!

- Sometimes what makes a cherry tomato variety taste best—its thin, tender skin—can also lead to problems. During periods of wet weather or high

humidity, cherry tomatoes have a tendency to split or crack on the vine. Prevent this problem by keeping moisture levels constant. A sudden influx of water on dry soil results in tomatoes swelling and splitting their skins. Cracked fruit soon rots, so pick and throw fruit with split skins away; they should not be eaten.

*A colourful selection of cherry tomatoes makes an attractive salad.*

- Generally, cherry tomatoes have fewer problems with blossom-end rot, scarring, distorted or misshapen fruit and insect pests than do larger tomatoes.

- One of the nicest things about cherry tomatoes is that you can pick them as soon as they start to ripen. Just-ripened tomatoes have a tang that you won't find in riper ones. I like to pick the fruit as soon as it turns colour. This also minimizes problems with fruit cracking or splitting on the vine.

My daughter-in-law Valerie says cherry tomatoes have a tang not found in larger tomatoes. She often slices these tasty morsels for sandwiches.

In an effort to provide better-tasting supermarket tomatoes, a Dutch company plans to ship small clusters or bunches of fully ripened tomatoes, still on the vine. These vine-ripened tomatoes would have fully developed flavour, unlike those now found in grocery stores, which are harvested green.

Cherry tomatoes generally mature a couple of weeks earlier than larger tomatoes, providing an extended harvest and a guarantee of ripe tomatoes in areas with very short growing seasons.

Ever wonder why people grew tomatoes in the days when they were afraid to eat them? Although tomatoes were commonly considered poisonous, they were still admired for their beauty and versatility. Tomatoes were used to make green and orange dyes, to remove ink and fruit stains from linen, to deter pests, cure scours in pigs and to feed hogs, domestic fowl and cattle. It was believed that tomato-fed cows produced more milk and a finer-flavoured butter. (A note of caution here: go ahead and feed green or overripe tomatoes to livestock, but don't give them tomato leaves or stems. They are poisonous to humans, and have been known to cause death in animals.)

# Bruschetta

*'A surprisingly easy recipe, guaranteed to stimulate even the discerning palate. Enjoy.'*

—Brian Green, c.c.c., Executive Chef de Cuisine, Westin Hotels & Resorts

12 oz. tomato concasse (coarsely chopped or ground tomatoes)
1 oz. basil, chopped
1 oz. Italian parsley, chopped
2 oz. garlic, chopped, cooked
4 oz. Parmesan cheese
4 large slices basil bread (available at many bakeries)
¼ cup olive oil
salt & pepper

Sauté off the garlic in olive oil. Add tomato, basil and parsley; warm. Remove from heat. Place in bowl. Toss in the Parmesan. Taste for seasoning. Serve on toasted basil bread. Serves 4.

# PASTE TOMATOES

*'...great for making sauces...'*

Most people think of paste tomatoes as 'sauce toma-toes,' or as they are commonly called at grocery stores, Roma tomatoes. Roma is actually a variety and not a type of tomato, and although it is the best-known variety, it is not necessarily the best variety to grow. One of our best customers comes out to the green-houses every spring to buy paste tomato plants. The first year that we switched from the variety Roma to the variety Mamma Mia, he didn't want to try it. I said that I would give him two plants to try, on the condi-tion that he label the Mamma Mia plants and grow them alongside the Roma, as a comparison. The next year he was back, and bought 96 Mamma Mias and no Romas!

*Some people think of paste tomatoes as being only for cooking, but Mamma Mia is one of my favourite toma-toes for salads.*

Paste tomatoes are a great choice for people who like their tomatoes meaty and flavourful, with few seeds.

## What Makes a
## Paste Tomato Different?

- Not all paste tomatoes are pear- or plum-shaped; some are round. The difference between paste and other tomatoes is not shape, but what is on the inside. Paste tomatoes are meatier and less juicy, with high sugar and acid contents that contribute to great flavour.

For a delicious, full-bodied tomato juice, use a few paste tomatoes along with the other varieties.

- Paste tomatoes are typically 5–6 per cent higher in pectin than other tomatoes are, resulting in a thicker sauce. Slicing tomatoes, even when cooked down, produce a thinner sauce.

# RECOMMENDED VARIETIES

### MAMMA MIA

- More than twice the yield of other paste varieties; incredible numbers of delicious, 3- to 4-oz. (85–113 g) tomatoes; excellent for canning and sauces, but also wonderful for fresh eating!

- Determinate, hybrid; 62 days to maturity. Use cage, do not prune.

- Use a strong cage to support Mamma Mia plants. One of our plants was so heavy with tomatoes that it bent over its cage! You may need to add a couple of stakes for additional support.

- Because of its heavy yield, Mamma Mia needs lots of water and fertilizer.

*Donna Dawson was pleased with the yield from her Mamma Mia. From a single plant, expect to harvest about 20 lbs. (9 kg) of tomatoes.*

## Other Comparable Varieties

*La Roma*: a hybrid of Roma, with larger fruit and earlier maturity than the original; heavy yields of good-tasting, 3- to 4-oz. (85–113 g) plum-shaped tomatoes; hybrid, determinate; 62 days to maturity.

*Roma*: the best-known paste tomato, so popular that its name has become synonymous with the paste type of tomato; 2-oz. (57 g), bright red, plum-shaped tomatoes; developed by the U.S. Department of Agriculture in 1955; open-pollinated, determinate; 75 days to maturity.

*San Marzano*: also known as Italian Canner; the original Italian paste variety from which Roma was bred as an improvement; matures later and has drier, more rectangular, larger fruits; average size 4 oz. (113 g); open-pollinated, indeterminate; 80 days to maturity.

*When harvesting tomatoes from Mamma Mia, remember to check for fruit hidden behind its bushy leaves.*

*One Mamma Mia plant bears about 25 clusters of tomatoes; be sure to use a strong cage to keep plants upright.*

**Saucy:** heavy yield of blunt-ended, 3-oz. (85 g) plum-shaped tomatoes in clusters of 5–10; matures later than Mamma Mia; open-pollinated, determinate; 75 days to maturity.

**Viva Italia:** sets fruit well in hot weather; tomatoes average 3 oz. (85 g); very disease-resistant; hybrid, determinate; 75 days to maturity.

Most paste tomatoes are less prone to blossom-end rot than most other tomato types.

The finest tomato wine is said to taste like a good, medium-sweet sherry. Reputedly, the best variety for wine-making is an heirloom called 'Riesentraube.' The name translates to 'large grape,' an apt description of this unique Austrian tomato, different from all other tomato plants because it bears sprays of 200–300 flowers, and clusters of 20–40 small tomatoes with pointed ends.

# NOVELTY TOMATOES

*'...a surprising range of colour...'*

Almost everyone would colour a picture of a tomato red, but tomatoes actually come in a surprising range of colours. The full palette includes orange, yellow, pink and white; there are some that remain green when ripe, and others that mature to a curious brownish-black. Some have stripes, some have skins of one colour and flesh of another, and some have surprising shapes, resembling a pear or a bell pepper. How do these novelties taste? Most taste great, and despite their un-tomato-like looks, not all that different from red, home-grown tomatoes.

At a state fair in the 1960s, about 3,000 people partici-pated in a taste test comparing a red and an orange tomato variety. The majority chose the red tomatoes as best tasting, until a blind taste-test was performed. Once people could no longer see the colour, it became a split decision on which tomato was better-tasting.

*Although not generally classed as a novelty tomato, Oxheart is unusual-looking, with its heart shape and pink colour.*

# WHAT MAKES A RED TOMATO RED?

- Red colouring comes from a high concentration of a hydrocarbon called lycopene.

- Orange tomatoes have a high concentration of beta-carotene, the same pigment that gives other vegetables, such as carrots, their colour.

- Yellow tomatoes also have high amounts of beta-carotene. The first tomatoes grown in Italy were yellow, hence the name *pomo d'oro* —'golden apple'—although yellow tomatoes have since become less common.

- Pink tomatoes have red flesh like most tomatoes. Their hue is softened to pink by translucent skin.

- White tomatoes have translucent skin over pale yellow flesh, which makes them appear to be creamy white.

Mild taste is often due to fewer seeds rather than colour; flavour compounds are concentrated in the gel around the seeds. Many novelty tomatoes are milder-tasting than red ones because their meaty interiors have few seeds.

About 50 years ago, tomato varieties with stout central stems and bushy, upright growth, such as Heartland and Patio, were commonly called 'tree tomatoes.' If you see that term used today, it likely refers to the tamarillo (*Cyphomandra betacea*), also called 'tree tomato,' a sub-tropical evergreen tree up to 8 feet (2.5 m) tall that bears small, hard, tart fruits used in preserves, salsas, relishes and sweet or savoury sauces. The taste is said to be a pleasingly bitter cross between tomatoes and apricots. Tamarillos are in the same botanical family (Solanaceae) as tomatoes.

## BETTER BUSH PINK

- sweet, juicy, pink tomatoes on a bushy plant similar to Heartland (see page 66); looks nice enough to grow in flowerbeds; tomatoes average 4–8 oz. (113–227 g); good disease-resistance; determinate, hybrid; 70 days to maturity.

## EVERGREEN

- heirloom variety also known as Emerald Evergreen; said to be the best-flavoured green tomato; beefsteak tomatoes remain rich olive-green inside and out, turning a brighter shade of green with a golden yellow tint when ripe; average fruit size 8–10 oz. (227–284 g); very good, mild, sweet flavour; good for slicing, frying and conserves; indeterminate, open-pollinated; 72 days to maturity.

## GREAT WHITE

- big white beefsteak with mild, sweet flavour and few seeds; average tomato size 10–12 oz. (284–340 g), larger than White Beauty; vigorous plants with heavy foliage that protects from sun-scald; heirloom variety; indeterminate, open-pollinated; 85 days to maturity.

## GARDEN PEACH

- abundant clusters of small to medium-sized yellow tomatoes with a pink blush and slightly fuzzy skin, like peaches; mild flavour; average fruit size 4–6 oz. (113–170 g); heirloom variety, the original long-keeping tomato; indeterminate, open-pollinated; 80 days to maturity.

## MR. STRIPEY

- an heirloom variety also known as Tigerella; huge crop of small red tomatoes with golden stripes; even unripe fruit is attractively striped in dark green; average tomato size 3–4 oz. (85–113 g),  2 inches (5 cm); rich, tangy and juicy; use whole or sliced for interesting salads; indeterminate, open-pollinated; 56 days to maturity.

## ORANGE QUEEN

- bright orange, mild-flavoured tomatoes; average 6 oz. (170 g); good for canning; compact plants; determinate, open-pollinated; 65 days to maturity.

## PINK GRAPEFRUIT

- unusual tomatoes with yellow skins and blush-pink interiors; delicious, sweet, mild flavour; average fruit size 5–6 oz. (142–170 g); indeterminate, open-pollinated; 70 days to maturity.

## TANGERINE

- heirloom variety with deep yellow-orange beefsteak tomatoes; heavy yields; meaty fruit with sweet, rich flavour; average size 7–8 oz. (198–227 g); indeterminate, open-pollinated; 80–85 days to maturity.

## TIGERETTE CHERRY

- red and yellow striped, small, plum-shaped tomatoes; average size 2 ¾ inches (7 cm); dwarf plants with ornamental yellowish-green foliage; determinate, hybrid; 68 days to maturity.

## WHITE BEAUTY

- heirloom variety with beefsteak tomatoes that are creamy white, inside and out; in my area, yields are rather low; high sugar content; very sweet, mild flavour; meaty tomatoes with few seeds, average about 8 oz. (227 g); indeterminate, open-pollinated; 85 days to maturity.

## YELLOW PEAR

* popular heirloom variety introduced in 1865; abundant clusters of small, lemon-yellow, pear-shaped tomatoes; mild flavour; average fruit size 1 oz. (28 g), about 2 inches (5 cm) long and 1 inch (2.5 cm) across; tall, vigorous vines; indeterminate, open-pollinated; 80 days to maturity.

## YELLOW STUFFER

* golden yellow tomatoes that look like bell-peppers, in both shape and in having hollow inside cavities; a great tomato for stuffing, but also very sweet when dried; average fruit size 6 oz. (170 g); indeterminate, open-pollinated; 80 days to maturity.

## The Tryst

'Potato was deep in the dark underground,
Tomato above in the light.
The little tomato was ruddy and round
The little potato was white.
And redder and redder she rounded above
And paler and paler he grew
And neither suspected a mutual love
Til they met in a Brunswick Stew.'
— *written in the late 19th century by John B. Tabb,*
*Episcopal minister, Amelica County, Virginia*

*No longer do these two vegetables have to wait to meet in the kitchen, for a tomato plant and a potato plant can be grafted together and called...a potomato. The grafted plant will produce potato tubers and tomato fruit, allowing two kinds of plant to be grown in the space it takes for one. Although I've talked to several people who have had quite good success with these grafted plants, I feel that the potomato is more of a novelty, but still well worth a try!*

# TOMATILLOS & GROUND CHERRIES

*'...they have a place in my garden every year...'*

*Tomatillo is a Mexican word, pronounced 'tome-ah-tee-yo.'*

*Physalis ixocarpa:*
Tomatillo
Husk Tomato
Mexican Green Tomato
Tomate Verde

*Physalis peruviana:*
Ground Cherry
Cape Gooseberry
Golden Berry
Strawberry Tomato

Tomatillos and ground cherries are wonderful plants for those who like to experiment with something different in both the garden and kitchen. I first tried them about four years ago, and liked them so much that I will definitely continue to give both tomatillos and ground cherries a place in my garden every year. Grow them just like tomatoes, with lots of sun, water and fertilizer. Tomatillos resemble firm, lustrous, green cherry tomatoes, with a distinctive, tangy taste that some say hints of apple, lemon and herbs. Ground cherries look more like golden marbles and have a unique flavour, like a blend of tomato, strawberry, grape and gooseberry.

The fruits of tomatillos and ground cherries are hidden inside inflated papery seedpods, like those of the Chinese Lantern plant (Physalis alkekengii), a perennial commonly grown for its ornamental orange seedpods. Tomatillos and ground cherries belong to the same botanical family as tomatoes, and seed catalogues usually list tomatillos and ground cherries within or just after their tomato sections.

*Ground cherries add unique flavour to fruit salad.*

*Tomatillos and ground cherries are easy to grow and produce heavy yields of tasty fruit that you can eat right off the vine.*

# RECOMMENDED VARIETIES

## TOMATILLO

- Indian Strain: early-maturing fruit with a very sweet flavour.
- Mexican Strain: larger, more savoury fruit; heavy yields.

## GROUND CHERRY

- Aunt Molly's: the cleanest, richest, most fruity flavour of all varieties, golden-orange fruit drops to ground when ripe.

# WHEN TO PLANT

Seeding: Sow indoors later than tomatoes—about four weeks before transplanting into the garden. Follow the directions for 'Starting Tomatoes from Seed' on page 18.

Transplanting: Plant outdoors when you plant your tomatoes—about one to two weeks after the average last spring frost. (See chart on pages 37 and 38.)

# GROWING TIPS

- Plant in a sunny location with light, well-drained soil. A warm, sheltered location near a heat-reflecting wall results in an earlier harvest.
- Tomatillos grow about 4–5 feet (120–150 cm) tall. Space plants 2–3 feet (60–90 cm) apart. You can grow either with or without support. I prefer a trellis because it makes it easier to work around the plants and pick the fruit. Branch tips can be pruned to control the plant's spread.
- Ground cherries grow 1–2 feet (30–60 cm) tall, but are wide-spreading. Space about 3 feet (90 cm) apart.
- Keep well-watered and fertilize regularly, just like tomatoes!

*Tomatillos are wide-spreading plants that do best in a sunny site.*

• Cover plants whenever there is a risk of frost.

# HARVESTING

## TOMATILLO

• Expect to begin harvesting 55–65 days after transplanting.

• Harvest when fruit grows large enough to split husks. Depending on variety, ripe fruit may be green or pale yellow.

### GROUND CHERRY

• Expect to begin harvesting 65–70 days after transplanting.

• Harvest when husks are tan-coloured and fruits yellow, gold or orange. With some varieties, ripe fruits drop to the ground.

*Tomatillos are a good source of vitamins C and K, and are low in calories. Ground cherries are high in vitamin C. Both of these plants are rarely troubled by pests.*

# COOKING IDEAS

## TOMATILLO

• Tomatillos go great with chili peppers, onions, garlic and cilantro!

• Add tomatillos to salsa, taco sauces, cheese dishes, guacamole, potatoes, chicken and Mexican dishes.

• Usually, tomatillos are cooked before eating but they can also be eaten raw. To cook, simmer for 5–10 minutes.

• Tomatillos can be substituted for, or combined with, tomatoes, in many recipes that call for tomatoes alone. Experiment to find your favourites!

• Tomatillos can be used when they are still green.

## GROUND CHERRY

- Use as you would any fruit: eaten fresh, raw or cooked, in desserts, sweet sauces, preserves, fruit toppings, pies or salads.

- This versatile fruit can also be stewed with meat, made into jams, or dipped in chocolate for a delightful dessert. Add some to apple pies, or chop and mix in muffins.

Ground cherries are also called Cape gooseberries.

- Ground cherries make a great 'palate freshener' in the middle of a rich meal.

- Use only golden ground cherries; green ones are not ripe.

## PREPARATION

- Remove ground cherry husks by opening up and twisting at the base to release fruit.

- Before using, rinse well to remove sticky residue.

## STORING

- Both tomatillos and ground cherries have amazing storage life, lasting up to a month in the refrigerator. Left inside their husks, ground cherries keep for up to three months!

- Store in a paper-lined open dish in the fridge. Ground cherries are best kept in a single layer.

- Tomatillos freeze well, once cooked. Barely cover peeled, washed tomatillos with water and simmer until softened. Leave in water to cool, and freeze with water in 1 cup (250 ml) increments for handy sauce-making. Use both liquid and fruit in sauces.

*The most common use for tomatillos is in Mexican salsas, but they also add piquant flavour to meats, sauces, casseroles and pies.*

# Salsa Verde

*Tomatillos have been called the secret ingredient
for a great salsa.*

> —Judy Barrett, *Tomatillos: A Gardener's Dream,
> A Cook's Delight.*

1 lb. tomatillos
1 cup chopped onion
4 cloves garlic
1 ½ teaspoons salt
½ cup oil
1 cup water
¼ cup cilantro (or to taste)
2 serrano peppers (or to taste)

Cut tomatillos in half and place in blender or food processor with
other ingredients. Blend until well chopped and mixed, but not wa-
tery. Pour into heavy pan and simmer on low heat for 10–12 minutes.
Serve as a dip, use in a recipe, or freeze.

Hot peppers can cause severe skin and eye irritation. Wear rubber
gloves when handling hot peppers and avoid touching exposed skin.

# Salad of Avocado,
# Cape Gooseberries, and Cucumber

*Buttery avocados suit tart Cape gooseberries as they do tomatoes.
Use the hothouse of English cucumber (or seedless, burpless—whatever they're called in your market) for the good texture its sweet-
tasting skin and crisp flesh provide.*

> —Elizabeth Schneider, *Uncommon Fruits
> & Vegetables: A Commonsense Guide.*

*4–5 servings.*

½ large English cucumber
7-ounce container Cape gooseberries, husked and rinsed, halved
2 medium avocados
2 tablespoons lemon juice
½ teaspoon coarse kosher salt, or to taste
pepper to taste
6 tablespoons olive oil
¼ cup finely chopped fresh cilantro
small bunch watercress, well trimmed, rinsed and dried

1. Trim off tips and quarter cucumbers lengthwise. Cut across in thin
   slices. Combine in bowl with gooseberries.

2. Halve and seed avocados. With small melon-ball cutter remove flesh
   and add to bowl.

3. Mix lemon juice, salt, and pepper. Add oil and blend well. Pour
   over salad, add cilantro and mix well.

4. Serve on a bed of watercress.

# TOMATO MANIA

**THE TOMATO FRESH FOOD CAFÉ** in Vancouver, B.C. has served over a quarter of a million tomatoes since it opened in 1991. Among the most popular items on their menu are the Tomato's Tomato, a nineties' version of the BLT, and Campbell's canned tomato soup. Why the name? 'Somehow this image of a bright, vibrant, ripe, juicy, almost voluptuous fruit symbolized everything we envisioned for our diner,' explains owner and chef Diane Clement in her most recent cookbook, *Diane Clement at the Tomato*.

**THE GREAT TOMATO WORKS** in Ohio is a 2,100-square-foot (195 m²) scientific exhibit at Lake Farmpark, Kirtland. It features a gigantic tomato plant with an 18-inch-wide (45 cm) stem, 12-foot-long (3.75 m) leaves and 6-foot-wide (180 cm) tomatoes. Visitors can learn about insects, photosynthesis, pollination, hydroponics and ketchup-making.

# HOW TO PLANT
*'...build a dam...'*

# HOW TO TRANSPLANT TOMATOES

*1) Prepare a hole for each plant. Pinch off some of the lower leaves and place plants into the holes, just slightly deeper than they were growing in their original containers.*

*2) Deep planting is best, because roots will form along any part of the stem that is buried, resulting in a stronger plant. Refill planting hole with soil, and pack the soil down firmly with your hands.*

*3) Use your hands to build a rim of soil about 3 inches (7.5 cm) high and 1 foot (30 cm) across, encircling the plant. This creates a 'dam' to hold water around the plant.*

*4) Water immediately, until the dam is completely filled. Fertilize now, and once a week for the next two weeks using a water-soluble fertilizer with a high middle number, such as 10-52-10. Add cages or stakes now. See 'Staking & Caging' on page 104.*

Space plants 3–4 feet (90–120 cm) apart. Allow about 3 feet (90 cm) between rows for maximum yield. If you have limited space, don't worry! You can plant as close as 18 inches (45 cm), but yields may be lower.

Deep planting results in increased early yields and larger tomatoes, according to an article in *American Vegetable Grower* magazine, based on a recent study in Florida. Tomatoes planted at the first true-leaf depth yielded 60% more tomatoes than those planted at rootball depth, with over twice as many extra-large tomatoes at first harvest. Later in the season, yields between the two evened out.

# HOW TO TRENCH-PLANT TOMATOES

For long-stemmed and lanky, plants trench-planting is the best method.

*1) Pinch off the lower leaves, taking care not to damage the main stem. Instead of a hole, dig a 'trench' about 2–4 inches (5–10 cm) deep and 8 inches (20 cm) long.*

*2) Lay the entire plant horizontally into the trench. Cover the stem with soil, leaving just the top cluster of leaves above the surface. Roots will form all along the buried stem, enabling the plant to better absorb water and nutrients. Since more roots are formed near the warm soil surface, the plants quickly become vigorous, resulting in increased yields and earlier maturity.*

*3) Refill the trench with soil, and pack down firmly with your hands. The plant will be laying almost completely sideways at this point but don't worry.*

*4) Build a dam to hold water (see step 3, opposite). Water immediately, until the dam is completely filled. Fertilize now, and once a week for the next two weeks using a water-soluble fertilizer with a high middle number, such as 10-52-10.*

*5) Add cages or stakes now. Take care when inserting the stake not to put it on the 'root side' of the plant! Within a few days, you will notice the plant has straightened up.*

# STAKING & CAGING

*'...easier to pick...'*

*As your plants grow, tie them to stakes.*

*I always tell gardeners to stake or cage their tomatoes. If you don't, some of the fruit will invariably get attacked by slugs, mice or soil-borne diseases. Staked or caged plants take up less space in the garden, are easier to work around, and the fruit is easier to pick and often ripens earlier. I find that a lot fewer branches break when I pick the fruit from a staked or caged plant than from a sprawling plant, and honestly, there is nothing more disheartening than breaking off a beautiful fruit-laden branch!*

# HOW TO STAKE

- Put stakes in immediately after transplanting. Drive them about 1 foot (30 cm) deep in the soil, approximately 3–5 inches (7.5–12.5 cm) away from the plant. If you have trench-planted tomatoes, do not put the stake on the root side of the plant (see 'How to Trench-plant Tomatoes' on page 103).

- Set stakes on the opposite side of the prevailing winds for your area. This way, plants will be moved toward the supports in strong winds.

- As each plant grows, tie it loosely to the stake. Use a soft material that won't damage the stem. You can buy foam-covered wire plant-ties, or cut old nylon stockings into strips. Leave 1–2 inches (2.5–5 cm) of slack to allow the stem to thicken and grow. Add more ties as plants grow taller.

One creative gardener built a 'tee-pee' of four stakes and planted three or four different tomato varieties around it. It was especially interesting because the tomatoes were different sizes and colours—cherry, small and medium-sized tomatoes of red, orange and yellow—great for making a colourful salad!

*By staking your indeterminate tomato plants, you can grow two or even three plants in the space required by a single unstaked plant.*

# HOW TO CAGE TOMATOES

- Set cages over the tomatoes immediately after transplanting. Push the cages firmly into the ground.

- For bigger tomato plants or very vigorous varieties, peony rings (as they are called) are better than tomato cages because they are taller and wider.

*Uncaged or free-growing tomato plants take up more space in the garden than those that are supported. Add cages or stakes immediately after transplanting.*

*Make the most of your garden space by growing vegetables that need less sun, such as leaf lettuce, beneath staked tomatoes.*

# Roasted Tomato Consommé

*'A light, refreshing and nutritious soup for summer.'*

—Timothy Wood, culinary arts instructor, Northern Alberta Institute of Technology

1 large onion, chopped
2 celery stalks with leaves, chopped
1 carrot, chopped
1 red bell pepper, seeded and chopped
2 garlic cloves
15 whole plum tomatoes
1 litre vegetable stock
2 tbsp. fresh basil, chopped
1 tbsp. fresh tarragon, chopped
1 tsp. fresh chives, chopped
1 tsp. fresh thyme, chopped
1 tsp. fresh oregano, chopped
fresh black pepper
salt

Place onions, carrot, celery and garlic in a medium roasting pan and place in a 400°F oven for 1 hour, checking periodically and stirring. The vegetables should be slightly browned. Meanwhile, preheat a barbeque grill until very hot and lightly coat tomatoes with olive oil, place on grill and roast until almost charred. Remove tomatoes from grill and vegetables from oven and place all vegetables into a medium stock pot. Add the vegetable stock and simmer until all the vegetables are very tender, about 1 hour. Stir in the herbs and simmer for another ½ hour. Strain through 4 layers of cheesecloth. Garnish and serve.
Yield: 1 litre.

This soup is very refreshing, light and low in fat and contains no cholesterol.

# WATERING

*'...whoever controls the water controls the profit...'*

*Dave Grobel collects rainwater in a 200-gallon tank, and uses only that for water his garden.*

I remember attending a horticultural conference a few years ago. A management consultant addressing the audience said that, in her opinion, even a six-year-old child could take care of watering plants. I strongly disagree. Yes, a child can water plants but he or she may not water them properly. There is a saying in the greenhouse industry that 'whoever controls the watering controls the profit.' Plants that are watered well will be healthy and strong, and they will continue to flourish in times of stress while other plants succumb.

With tomato plants, inadequate watering quickly becomes obvious: leaves droop and plants wilt. When a tomato plant receives a fluctuating water supply, meaning that soil is alternately allowed to dry and then is soaked, its fruit often suffers. Blossom-end rot—those mushy, brown or black spots on the bottom of ripening fruit still on the vine—is one of the most common results. Ripening tomatoes can also split or crack as a result of improper watering.

## HOW TO WATER PROPERLY

- Water heavily every day without fail if the weather is hot and dry. Aim the water at the ground, not the foliage.

- An even, adequate supply of water is most important when tomatoes are first forming. Inconsistent watering (allowing the plant to dry out and then

The average tomato is 95% water. What makes the difference in flavour is the remaining 5%—a combination of sugars, acids and about 400 other elements.

*Tomatoes are like people. You can't drink your whole week's supply of water on Monday and expect it to last the whole week. You need water every day, and it's the same with tomatoes.*

Cherry tomatoes are particularly susceptible to splitting after dry soil is drenched, such as during a summer thundershower. The fruit is unable to cope with the sudden influx of water, and cracking results. Regular watering helps keep your tomatoes intact.

soaking it) or too little watering can result in smaller fruit and blossom-end rot.

- Water deeply. Deep watering encourages deep roots, allowing plants to absorb moisture from deep in the soil even when the soil surface becomes dry or when you occasionally forget to water. A tomato plant's roots can grow about 4 feet (120 cm) deep.

- Water containers until they are full to the brim. Let the water soak in, and then water again, until moisture seeps from the drainage holes in the bottom of the pot.

Proper watering can result in twice as many tomatoes. Tomato plants that received water whenever they needed it had double the yields of those that became dry, according to a report in *The Tomato Club* newsletter, based on a study by the U.S. Department of Agriculture.

More water less often is better than less water more often. Heavy soaking actually uses less water than frequent light sprinkling, and it helps plants to develop stronger, deeper root systems.

# FERTILIZING

*'...a pinch a day...'*

*I firmly believe that nobody performs well on an empty stomach. Plants are no different, and tomatoes, in particular, need their 'breakfast' food to produce the best yields and best-quality fruit. I like the 'pinch-a-day' principle: a pinch of 20-20-20 fertilizer in your water every day will keep your tomatoes healthy all season long.*

## FERTILIZER BASICS

- Plants require three major nutrients in relatively large quantities: nitrogen, phosphorous and potassium. Even rich soils rarely contain an optimum supply for all vegetables. It is usually necessary to supplement. Tomatoes are classed as 'heavy feeders' so it is particularly important to provide additional nourishment.

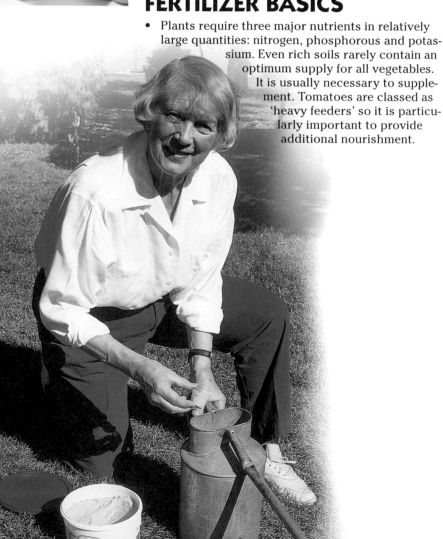

- The three numbers on fertilizer containers indicate the percentage of major nutrients by weight, always in the same order, N-P-K. For example, a 10-52-10 fertilizer contains a minimum of 10 per cent nitrogen, 52 per cent phosphate or phosphorous and 10 per cent potash or potassium.

- Nitrogen (N) promotes leafy plant growth and lush leaves; good organic sources are manure and blood-meal. Too much nitrogen produces excessive leaf and shoot growth, and actually reduces the yield of tomatoes.

- Phosphorous (P) promotes root development and flowering; good organic sources are bone-meal and rock phosphate. For best fruit development, tomatoes need a high-phosphate fertilizer.

- Potassium (K) promotes fruit quality and disease resistance; good organic sources include kelp-meal and manure.

- Tomatoes, like all plants, require micronutrients, elements such as zinc, boron and magnesium. In most gardens, these are usually present in sufficient amounts, so unless you have an unexplained problem with your plants, you needn't worry too much about them. See the chart on page 167 for symptoms of micronutrient deficiencies.

Need another good reason to use a 'plant-starter' fertilizer in spring? High phosphorous fertilizer increases frost tolerance in plants, while high-nitrogen fertilizer lowers it, according to Dr. Paul Ragan of Alberta Agriculture's research division.

*Although there are many factors that can cause tomato plants to bear little or no fruit, the three most common are too much nitrogen, low temperatures, and not enough sun.*

*Tricia Murray and her dad Wayne had great results with Super Fantastic.*

- Calcium is an exception. Most soils have adequate quantities of calcium, but it is difficult for plants to absorb the calcium and transport it to developing fruit. The only way to get calcium to the fruit is to 'push it through' with lots of water. Be sure to water regularly. Calcium is important for the proper development of roots and shoots, and is also essential for preventing blossom-end rot. Without calcium, cell walls collapse and fluids leak out, resulting in dark, mushy, rotten spots on tomatoes.

- Plants growing in containers should always be fertilized with a water-soluble fertilizer (see page 113) such as 20-20-20, in addition to or instead of granular fertilizer. A water-soluble fertilizer contains micronutrients, but neither potting mix nor granular fertilizers contain any at all.

# WHICH FERTILIZER IS BEST?

- I categorize fertilizers into two basic types: those you add directly to soil (granular) and those you mix with water first (water-soluble.)

- Some gardeners prefer granular fertilizers and some prefer the water-solubles. I use a combination of both, because I don't believe that granular fertilizers alone are adequate for keeping tomatoes growing at their best all season long, especially plants in containers. The water-solubles, I feel, are somewhat more fine-tuned to the plants' needs, and quantities can be increased or reduced as I see fit. This is impossible with granulars because they are usually mixed in the soil and dissolve slowly.

## Granular Fertilizers

- The simplest fertilizer to use is a spike which is pressed into the soil next to the plant right after planting. That's all you need to do! The fertilizer spike releases nutrients as plants require them. Be sure to choose one especially formulated for tomatoes.

- The best granular fertilizers are made up of slow-release fertilizer pellets which feed plants slowly over a long period of time. Work these into the soil before planting. A formula such as 5-10-15 is good for tomatoes.

## Water-soluble Fertilizers

- Water-soluble fertilizers produce quick results by rapidly releasing all their nutrients. These types are added to the watering can or dispersed through a fertilizer dispenser that attaches to the hose. For tomatoes, choose either a specific tomato food like 15-15-30 or an all-purpose fertilizer like 20-20-20.

- Immediately after transplanting, apply a high-phosphate fertilizer to aid in root development and help new plants adjust. These are often called 'plant-starter' fertilizers. I use 10-52-10 in the watering can, but another alternative is to mix bone-meal into the soil of the planting hole.

# HOW TO FERTILIZE TOMATOES

- Regular addition of organic matter, like compost or peat moss, helps. Usually, though, I find that the healthiest plants are those that are also fertilized regularly.

- If you are using granular fertilizer, mix it into the soil before transplanting tomatoes in spring. If you are using a fertilizer spike, push it into the soil just after transplanting.

- With water-soluble fertilizers, use a starter fertilizer such as 10-52-10 weekly for the first three weeks after transplanting. Thereafter, I recommend feeding tomatoes every time you water, with just a pinch of 20-20-20 fertilizer added to the watering can.

*Regular fertilizing greatly improves yields, and is especially important for container-grown plants.*

Fact or folklore: *Epsom salts aid the growth of tomato plants.*
Fact. Epsom salts are actually a fairly pure form of magnesium sulphate. Chlorophyll uses magnesium in the process of transforming light into energy and sugar. Sulphur is a key component of proteins, which affect a variety of plant processes.

# PRUNING

*'...an earlier harvest...'*

*Remove suckers with your fingers or a sharp knife.*

A funny thing happens when you prune an entire greenhouse full of tomato plants: you become a green thumb—literally. You will also have a couple of green fingers, and they will remain green for a few days despite lots of soap and water. Home gardeners, however, do not have the 'green thumb' problem because it happens only after pruning more than a few tomato plants. Digit discolouration aside, I like everything about pruning tomato plants, from the distinctive smell of the plants to the hands-on work, and the thought that this small effort—a moment or two per plant—will result in an earlier harvest of larger tomatoes.

## WHICH TOMATO PLANTS TO PRUNE

- Prune only indeterminate varieties—the ones that grow tall and usually need staking. If you do not prune an indeterminate variety, you will have large, sprawling plants with smaller tomatoes that mature slightly later in the season.

- Never prune a semi-determinate or determinate tomato plant. Pruning them will result in distorted plants with very few tomatoes.

Although I am not one to worry about stained hands, there is a lanolin-based commercial product which can be applied prior to pruning to prevent the 'green-thumb syndrome.'

*Tiny suckers can simply be 'rubbed out' with your fingers.*

# HOW TO PRUNE TOMATO PLANTS

- Pruning tomato plants simply means pinching off the shoots or 'suckers' that grow out from the stems, in the joint right above a leaf branch. If you catch shoots when they have just formed, you can simply rub them out with your thumb.

- Small suckers can usually be pinched off with your fingers; with ones that are a little larger you should use scissors or a sharp knife.

- If you leave a sucker to grow, it becomes another big stem and takes energy away from fruit production. Tomatoes usually ripen slightly earlier on pruned plants.

- Tomato plants grow very quickly when the weather is warm. New suckers are produced constantly. Prune at least twice a week during the peak of the growing season.

*My basic rule is: If a tomato plant grows tall, prune it; if it grows wide like a bush, don't. Both of these plants are the same determinate variety, but after the one on the left was mistakenly pruned, it became stunted and produced very few tomatoes.*

*To aid in ripening, you can 'top' indeterminate plants by removing the tip of the leader or main stem toward the end of the season.*

- Never prune above the top blossom cluster to avoid accidentally pruning out the 'leader' (main growing stem). Removing the leader prevents the plant from adding height and limits the potential yield. This is called 'topping' and is useful later in the season, but it is not something you want to do early on. See 'Stacking the Odds for Harvest' on page 125 for other methods of encouraging ripening.

- If you accidentally break off the leader or main stem while your tomato plant is still small, get a new plant, because the broken one will never amount to much. When a leader is broken off an indeterminate plant that is already a good size, you can choose one of the suckers nearest the top and let that side-shoot become the new leader. Determinate plants with broken leaders will simply bush sideways.

- Do not prune foliage, except to remove yellowing or brown leaves at the plant's base. Tomatoes do not need to be exposed to the sun in order to ripen; rather, it is the sun on the plant's leaves that leads to ripened fruit.

## My Favourite Tomato Is...

'Whopper is the perfect hamburger tomato—large, firm, round with low seed count—a favourite of mine.'

—Mark Cullen, author, and President of Weall & Cullen Nurseries Limited, North York, Ontario

# Tomato & Fennel Seed Chutney

*'A versatile dish for a barbeque in summer, with antipasto or a roast in winter—you can use chutney with everything!'*

—Willie White, Executive Chef,
Hotel Macdonald,
Canadian Pacific Hotels & Resorts

14 tomatoes (fine dice)
2 Bermuda onions (fine dice)
2–3 oz. grated ginger
500 ml champagne vinegar
2 cups brown sugar
1 oz. fennel seed
pinch cayenne pepper
salt and pepper to taste

Heat a small saucepan and add vinegar, brown sugar and fennel seed. Boil rapidly for five minutes. Add onion, tomato, ginger, cayenne pepper. Turn back heat so mixture simmers. Stir every five or so minutes. Remove from heat when liquid is almost gone and mixture has thickened somewhat. Add salt and pepper to taste. Makes 1.5 litres.

# THE HOME GREENHOUSE

*'...from seed to harvest...'*

*A lot of the things we do in the garden, such as using hot caps, row covers, and putting plastic wrap around tomato cages, are an attempt to provide the benefits of a greenhouse. Most of the tomatoes I grow now spend their entire lives, from seed to harvest, inside the protective, controlled environment of a greenhouse or cold frame. If you already have or plan to install a greenhouse in your backyard, great! Here are some tips to help you grow the best greenhouse tomatoes.*

## RECOMMENDED GREENHOUSE VARIETIES

### COUNTER

- An exceptional variety for heavy yields of perfect, round, medium-sized tomatoes; average size 3–5 oz. (85–142 g); great resistance to blossom-end rot; open growth habit makes vines easy to work with; extremely popular in Europe.

- Indeterminate, hybrid; 60 days to maturity. Stake and prune.

If you are growing tomatoes in a container, ensure that there are sufficient drainage holes in the bottom of the container.

## VENDOR

- The best-tasting greenhouse tomato, in my opinion; large, thin-skinned fruit are sweet and juicy and have a tangy 'green tomato' taste even when ripe; very flavourful, 6–8 oz. (170–227 g) fruit.

- Indeterminate, open-pollinated; 70 days to maturity. Stake and prune.

## Other Comparable Greenhouse Varieties

**Cobra**: a greenhouse tomato with field-ripened flavour; lots of large, firm, tasty, 8-oz. (227 g) beefsteak tomatoes; indeterminate, hybrid; 75 days to maturity.

**Trust**: good yields of large, firm, round tomatoes; average size 8 oz. (227 g); vigorous plants; indeterminate, hybrid; 75 days to maturity.

*Bert Clark (left) has grown tomatoes in his home greenhouse for 15 years. His favourite varieties are Celebrity and Vendor.*

*Some commercial growers use bumblebees (below) to help pollinate tomato plants growing inside greenhouses. You can use this idea in your garden by growing flowers near your tomatoes—it may improve the harvest in the end, and the flowers will certainly provide an attractive display throughout the season.*

# RAISING TOMATOES IN A HOME GREENHOUSE

- For best results, grow varieties that were bred specifically for greenhouse conditions. Other varieties can be grown inside a greenhouse, but they cannot match the yields of greenhouse types.

- The ideal temperature for greenhouse tomato plants is 21–24°C (70–75°F) during the day and 17–18°C (62–64°F) at night.

- In our greenhouse, we grow tomatoes in 5-gallon (23-litre) buckets with a support string wound around each plant and attached to the overhead support beams. Some other growers weave a 'fence' of string by placing a stake between every second plant, tying string to the first stake and then encircling every stake on down the row. At the end of the row, they retrace the pattern on the other side of the row, thus completing the fence. Either of these options can be modified for home greenhouses.

*Vendor is one of my favourite greenhouse tomatoes. I have grown it for years, with exceptional results.*

Good ventilation not only controls greenhouse temperatures, but also helps to improve air quality. Inside a poorly ventilated greenhouse, carbon dioxide levels often fall so low that plants actually stop growing! Carbon dioxide is so important for plants that some commercial greenhouse operators use carbon dioxide generators to increase levels inside their greenhouses. They report that this results in tomatoes maturing earlier and growing larger, with overall yields increasing, on average, from 15 to 55%. Because it is so valuable, carbon dioxide has been called 'the abandoned goldmine.'

*Trust (left) is a popular greenhouse variety.*

*Gently shake tomato plants (above) growing in greenhouses to assist pollination.*

# POLLINATING TOMATOES

- Don't forget pollination! Greenhouse-grown tomato plants are not exposed to natural pollinators such as wind and insects, and they may have poor yields or produce rough fruit if you do not hand-pollinate them.

- Tomato plants pollinate best at temperatures in a range from 21 to 27°C (70–80°F). Below 18°C (65°F), pollination is delayed and yields are lowered. Above 32°C (90°F), you will have fewer tomatoes.

# HOW TO HAND-POLLINATE

- Between 10 A.M. and 4 P.M., when pollen is shed most abundantly, shake each truss for one or two seconds using your hand, an electric toothbrush or equivalent.

- Do this every second day while tomato plants are blooming.

Tomatoes are the most popular greenhouse crop.

'Strategies grow initially like weeds in a garden, they are not cultivated like tomatoes in a hothouse.'

—business management advice from Henry Mintzberg, author of Mintzberg on Management: Inside Our Strange World of Organizations

# THE NUMBER ONE PROBLEM IN HOME GREENHOUSES

*Cobra produces tasty tomatoes in long trusses. Harvest them by cutting off the entire truss, and picking tomatoes as you need them.*

- When gardeners come to me to solve problems with their greenhouse-raised tomatoes, the cause is almost always the same—the greenhouse is too hot!

- High temperatures reduce pollination and inhibit fruit-set on tomato plants. At daytime temperatures above 32°C (90°F) and nighttime temperatures above 26°C (79°F), yield and quality decline rapidly.

- Excessively high temperatures in greenhouses are usually caused by poor ventilation. When it is 30°C (86°F) outside, temperatures will easily be 38°C (100°F) or more inside the greenhouse. Prevent overheating by ensuring that you have adequate ventilation, including roof vents or at least one good fan, on the end wall opposite the door. When the weather becomes hot, prop the greenhouse door open to allow airflow.

- On hot summer days before you head off to work in the morning, be sure to open the vents or turn on the fan, and prop open the door.

- A roof vent that opens automatically is an excellent investment. This type of vent is controlled by a gas-filled cylinder. When the air temperature is warm, the gas expands and pushes open the vent. When the air temperature is cool, the gas contracts and closes the roof vent.

With the exception of local vine-ripened tomatoes, local hothouse tomatoes are your best buy at the grocery store. The price may be slightly higher because of the costs of heating and lighting greenhouses in winter, but the flavour is much sweeter and the texture closer to home-grown tomatoes.

'Get out of the house! Meet your neighbours face to face! Grow tomatoes! Turn the computer off, for heaven's sake!'

—modern advice to those spending too much time online from Clifford Stoll, author of *Silicon Snake Oil*

# Margarita Pasta with Sautéed Chicken

*'This is one of everybody's traditional favourites.'*

—Chris Lehto, Kitchen Leader, Joey Tomato's Kitchen

Start with 20 fl. oz. of your favourite fresh,
    plain tomato sauce
2 tbsp. pepper
2 tbsp. salt
4 fl. oz. olive oil
4 small shallots, chopped
½ oz. fresh basil leaves, chopped
1 oz. fresh Parmesan cheese, grated
1 chicken breast, boneless, skinless, sliced
2 garlic cloves
2 tbsp. butter

Combine olive oil and shallots in saucepan. Sauté until shallots
are clear. Add to tomato sauce. Chop garlic, sauté in butter.
Add chicken, sauté on medium-high heat until golden brown.
Add tomato sauce, pepper, salt, basil and Parmesan cheese.
Bring to a simmer and place on a bed of your favourite pasta.
Serves 2 hungry *pisanos*!

# THE GREAT TOMATO RACE

*'...stack the odds in your favour...'*

Every year, toward the end of the season, the same question arises in the minds of many gardeners: which will come first, ripe tomatoes or frost? Fortunately, we will have harvested at least a few ripe tomatoes before frost strikes, but usually not all of them. And so the race between fruit and frost begins. The most common scenario is one or two nights of low temperatures and perhaps a light frost in late summer or early fall, followed by another few weeks of good weather. It makes sense to do everything in our power to stack the odds in our favour.

*Removing small tomatoes encourages the others to ripen.*

# STACKING THE ODDS FOR HARVEST

- While tomatoes are forming and starting to ripen on the vine, don't forget to water! Time and time again I've seen gardeners with fruit that has rotted from watering too little and too late. Long before the fruit rots, little brown or black spots form on the bottom of the tomato. This is called 'blossom-end rot.' If you see those spots, get out the hose and start watering immediately.

- Don't bother removing leaves from your plants. Tomatoes do not need to be exposed to sun in order to ripen; rather, it is the sun on the plant's leaves that causes the fruit to ripen.

- Late in the season, about three weeks before the end of summer, remove all flowers and all tiny tomatoes to allow your plant's energy to be devoted to ripening those tomatoes that are already a good size.

- If your plants are in containers, move them into the sunniest area.

- If your tomatoes are the indeterminate type—tall ones that need staking and pruning—'top' the plants by removing the growing tip and uppermost set of leaves.

*Topping indeterminate plants in late summer (below) promotes ripening of fruit, but removing leaves from plants can inhibit ripening. Tomatoes ripen faster with foliage left intact (left), and are also protected from sun-scald.*

# PROTECTING FROM FROST

- Don't rush! I often hear about people who hurry out to the garden to pick all their tomatoes the first time the weather forecast predicts a chance of frost. It's better to wait and cover the plants for a couple of nights. Quite often, the earliest frosts are followed by another few weeks of good weather.

- When there is a risk of overnight frost, cover your tomato plants with whatever is handy. I keep a stack of old blankets and sheets in our garage. Burlap, old towels or cardboard boxes work well too, but don't use plastic sheeting because it has virtually no insulation value. Leave plants covered until mid-morning.

- To protect hanging baskets from frost, take them down from their hooks and move them indoors overnight.

- When a heavy frost is certain, it is a tradition around our home for everyone to rush out into the garden that evening and pick all the remaining tomatoes.

## My Favourite Tomato Is...

'We've always loved Celebrity tomatoes. They are great-tasting and reliable.'

—*Phil and Dorothy Bartlett, Ocean View Farm, Nantucket, Maine*

# Tomato Soup Scented with Gin

*'This recipe always makes me remember my mother's kitchen.'*

—Perry Michetti, Sous Chef, Hilton International Hotels

50 g sliced mushrooms
50 g diced onion
5 g crushed garlic
½ litre crushed tomatoes
½ litre chicken stock
½ litre heavy cream
pinch basil
pinch thyme
pinch salt & pepper
3 oz. dry gin

- Sauté onions and garlic in a bit of butter.

- Add the crushed tomatoes and chicken stock. Simmer for 20–30 minutes.

- Add herbs and seasonings.

- Add gin and cream.

- Purée in food processor or blender for 5–10 minutes.

- Finally, sauté mushrooms in a small amount of butter and add to hot soup.

- Garnish with freshly chopped parsley. Serves 6 people.

# HARVESTING TOMATOES

*'...baskets full of big, ripe tomatoes...'*

*Harvest ripe tomatoes by gently breaking the stem just above the fruit, at the knuckle.*

One year, at the end of a particularly wonderful, warm growing season, the expected failed to happen—there was no early fall frost. All the plants in our garden continued to flourish, the flowers kept blooming and the tomatoes ripened so quickly that we could barely keep up with the picking. There were roughly 200 tomato plants in our vegetable garden that year, and we hired people to fill basket after basket with big, ripe tomatoes. Customers at our farm wanted green tomatoes for relish, but that year we could not provide them—as soon as the tomatoes sized up, they turned red almost overnight.

It was marvellous, and highly unusual for my part of the world, where nighttime temperatures usually drop significantly in the fall. I have never seen a fall like that before, but expect to again; even the oddest weather patterns have a way of repeating themselves. Most summers, however, I need to try to tip the odds in my favour for the best possible harvest.

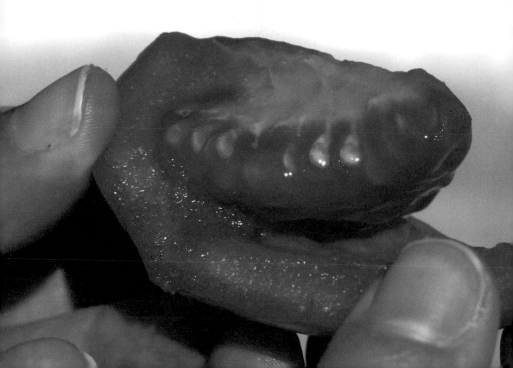

# HARVESTING TOMATOES

- I think tomatoes have the best flavour when they are picked just before they've reached their colour peak. At this stage, they are still firm and will last several days on your kitchen counter. Tomatoes that are already slightly soft will be at their best for only a day or two after picking.

- Red tomatoes left hanging on the vine will not taste as good as those harvested earlier, because the primary flavour components, sugar and acid, start to decrease.

- I always recommend that gardeners write on their garden calendars which varieties they like best. This certainly helps me out, because I sometimes find it tough to remember from year to year which of the new varieties were best.

- Harvest ripe tomatoes by gently breaking the stem just above the fruit at the knuckle. Always try to keep this bit of stem attached so that tomatoes will keep longer after picking.

- If your plant has an entire truss (branch-full) of ripe tomatoes, cut the whole thing off with scissors. An intact truss of tomatoes lasts longest of all!

*A basketful of freshly picked vegetables is sure to inspire cooks.*

*The optimum time to pick tomatoes is just as they are reaching their peak colour.*

*Try to keep a bit of stem attached when picking tomatoes. With stems attached, tomatoes lose moisture more slowly and stay fresh longer than those without stems.*

- Pick often to encourage the production of more fruit.

- If any of your tomatoes have developed blossom-end rot, pick them anyhow. Just cut off the rotten parts after harvesting—the remainder of the tomato is fine for eating. (Certain varieties, including Counter and Northern Exposure, are resistant to blossom-end rot.)

- A good friend told me of a 'harvesting' method which allowed her to keep on picking ripe tomatoes until early December. Try this if your container-grown plants are still bearing fruit at the end of the season. Move the entire pot into the garage, soil, plant and all, and don't do anything else to it, other than pick off ripe tomatoes as you need them. Don't worry about water or light. The plant will soon begin to look terrible but tomatoes will continue to ripen on the vine.

The Oldest Tomatoes in the World: In 1995, 2000-year-old tomato seeds were discovered inside a bamboo tube buried in a tomb in southwest China. Archaeologists wrapped the bamboo in a damp cloth to preserve it. To everyone's surprise, a month later, 40 tomato seeds had sprouted! They grew and yielded tomatoes with the same taste but a different shape than the tomatoes we grow today.

# SAVING TOMATO SEED

'You know Lois, I saved some seed from those great tomatoes I got from you two years ago. They didn't perform very well for me this year.' This is a story I've heard from more than one customer, and the reason for the lack of success is almost always the same: the seed was saved from a hybrid variety. Saving seeds from tomatoes is easy to do, but be sure that the seed is not from a hybrid variety. The best qualities of a hybrid plant usually exist only in the first generation. Seed collected from a hybrid plant is likely to produce a different plant of poorer quality.

🍅🍃 Properly stored, seed saved from tomatoes will remain viable for 1–10 years at room temperature.

With seed saved from open-pollinated heirloom tomato plants, however, gardeners can and do have wonderful results. Many gardeners grow tomatoes from seed that has been passed on in their family for generations. Some can identify the variety, while other people know only the tomato's origin—Italy, Germany or Russia.

🍅🍃 A tomato by any other name would still be ... a tomato. At various times throughout history, this famous fruit has been known as:

- love apple: a direct translation from the French *pomme d'amour*. At one time, tomatoes were believed to have aphrodisiacal qualities.

- *pomo d'oro*: an Italian name meaning 'golden apple,' still in use today. The first tomatoes taken to Europe were yellow or golden; this colour may also have led to the botanical name *Lycopersicon*; *persicon* is Latin for 'peach.'

- wolf peach: a literal translation from the Latin *Lycopersicon* (*lyco* for 'wolf,' *persicon* for 'peach'), the botanical name assigned to the tomato family in the 16th century after it was introduced to Europe. One theory for this name is that the tomato looked as inviting as a peach yet was as deadly as a wolf (at that time, tomatoes were still believed to be poisonous). The modern botanical name *Lycopersicon esculentum* means 'edible wolf peach.'

- *para disapfel*: a German name translating to 'apple of paradise.' Likely the same theory as the Latin: a tempting-looking fruit, a single bite of which would have dire consequences.

# HOW TO SAVE TOMATO SEED

If you save seed from tomatoes, be sure it is an open-pollinated variety. You won't get good results with seed from hybrid plants.

*1) Wash fully ripe tomatoes. Cut in half across middle—not through stem and blossom ends. Squeeze out seeds and gel into a plastic container or dish; use the rest of the tomato for eating or processing. It is easier to grind cherry tomatoes in a blender or food processor. Blend until mashed and mixture is very thick. The hard tomato seeds will not be damaged.*

*2) Add one cup (250 ml) water to each cup of mashed tomatoes.*

*3) Stir to separate the seeds. Put seeds into plastic containers. Warning: the containers will stink as contents ferment. Store them outside the house, in a spot where they will not be tipped over by children or animals. Stir twice daily.*

*4) After about three days, a thick layer of white or grey mould will form across the surface. This destroys the gel sac around each seed that prevents sprouting. When mould completely covers the surface, or you see bubbles rise in the mixture, stop the fermentation process. Left too long, the seeds will start to germinate.*

*5) Pour mixture into a sieve and run water through to clean, until only clean seeds remain. Remove moisture by wiping the outside of the sieve with a towel.*

*6) Spread seeds onto a glass or ceramic dish to dry. I use a clean coffee filter. Do not put seeds onto other types of paper, or onto cloth or plastic wrap, because they will stick to those.*

Place the seeds away from direct sunlight. Do not attempt to dry them in the oven. Stir at least twice a day to speed drying and prevent bunching. If it is hot and humid, use a fan to help drying and prevent germination.

Seal fully dried tomato seeds in airtight containers; label with date and variety, if known. Store in a cool, dry area.

'When you move into a new house, you should take with you three vegetables—tomatoes, lettuce and carrots—and some flowers, and you will always have plenty to eat and be happy.'

—folklore

## Salsa Fresca

*A delicious, no-cook salsa with a refreshing flavour and a nice kick.*

4 large ripe tomatoes, chopped
1 ½ medium white onions, peeled
    and finely chopped
6 fresh serrano chili peppers,
    finely chopped
1 cup cilantro, finely chopped
1 teaspoon oregano
juice of three limes
olive oil
salt to taste

Combine all ingredients and that's it—the salsa is done and ready to serve. Note: Wear gloves when chopping hot peppers, or use a blender or food-processor, to avoid transferring the 'heat' to your hands (it doesn't wash off with soap and water, and can irritate or burn sensitive skin).

# GREEN TOMATOES

*'...take advantage of the unripe fruit...'*

There comes a time when I tire of repeatedly covering and uncovering my tomato plants. At that point, daytime temperatures may be too cool for the plants to grow much more anyhow, so it is better to salvage whatever fruit there is and let the plants go. Green tomatoes ripen well indoors, but remember to take advantage of the unripe fruit in other ways too. My aunt always makes green tomato pickle, and my good friend Bob Manson thinks there is nothing in the world that compares to the taste of fried green tomatoes, an opinion that is shared by many others. In the years when we operated our market garden, many people came out looking for green rather than red tomatoes, and headed home with bushel baskets full of them. In fact, our late-season sales of green tomatoes often outnumbered the sales of ripe ones.

My family has eaten fried green tomatoes for years, at breakfast with bacon and eggs, and at dinner, served alongside pork.

# Chow Chow
# (Green Tomato Pickle)

*'My grandmother from Nova Scotia gave me this recipe. My favourite ways to eat it are with macaroni and cheese, meat, and fish such as cod and halibut.'*

—Mike MacDonald

10 lbs. green tomatoes, washed, sliced and put in large pot

Add ½ cup coarse salt and let stand all night with a weight on top.

In the morning, drain off the liquid and add:

1) 3 lbs. sliced onions

2) 5 cups white sugar

3) 2 or 3 chopped red peppers, 2 tbsp. dry mustard

4) 1 cup pickling spice, tied in a gauze bag or even a J-cloth. Remove bag when recipe is cooked.

5) 1 qt. vinegar.

Boil it gently until you like the taste. Add more sugar if you wish. Usually takes a ½ hour or so to cook. Not good to over-cook; it gets brownish.

Makes 6 great bottles. Ladle into hot, sterilized jars, leaving ½ inch (1.25 cm) headspace. Remove air bubbles with a spatula. Wipe jar rims thoroughly. Seal and process in a boiling water bath for 15 minutes.

# HOW TO RIPEN GREEN TOMATOES INDOORS

- Green tomatoes ripen better in the dark than in light, so the common practice of lining your windowsill with unripened tomatoes is not the best thing to do. In our old farmhouse, the master bedroom was just a few steps down the hall from our kitchen, so I used to keep ripening tomatoes under the bed.

- Place green tomatoes in a single layer between full sheets of newspaper. I like to use full sections, because the thickness allows me to pick up a whole layer of tomatoes while searching for ripened tomatoes underneath. With this method, tomatoes start to ripen in about a week.

- For faster ripening, place green tomatoes inside paper bags with an apple. Apples release ethylene gas, which causes tomatoes to turn red. (Ethylene gas is given off naturally by tomatoes when they ripen on the vine.)

*Folklore has it that tomatoes on the windowsill bring prosperity to the house, but the truth is that tomatoes ripen better in the dark than in light.*

*The tangy flavour of green tomatoes can be enjoyed in all sorts of appetizing dishes.*

## Green Tomato Mincemeat

*'Friends love my mincemeat tarts, but you should see their faces when I tell them the main ingredient is green tomatoes!'*

—June Raven

6 cups green tomatoes
4 cups apples (approx. 12)
3 cups raisins (1 lb.)
1 cup butter
1 tbsp. cinnamon
¾ cup vinegar
1 cup mixed peel or fruit
4 cups brown sugar
¾ tsp. allspice

Put tomatoes through food chopper. Put raisins and apples through food chopper separately. Cover tomatoes with water, boil, drain, repeat twice using fresh water. Add everything else. Bring to boil. Cook slowly 1 hour until mixture is clear & thick. Bottle. Yield: 10–12 pint jars.

## Barbequed Green Tomato Stir-Fry

Blue Flame Kitchen

2 cloves garlic, crushed
5 ml oil
1 small onion, sliced
3 sliced green tomatoes
1 ripe tomato, cut into wedges
5 ml basil
1 ml salt
0.5 ml pepper
0.5 ml sugar

Place wok directly on lava rock in gas barbeque. Over medium heat, sauté garlic in oil for one minute. Add onion and green tomatoes and stir-fry until vegetables are tender, about 5 minutes. Add ripe tomato and seasonings; heat through, about 2 minutes. Serves 4.

Note: Halved cherry tomatoes may be substituted for the ripe tomato.

# STORING AND PRESERVING TOMATOES

*'...make the most of your harvest...'*

After working and waiting all season to harvest luscious, vine-ripened tomatoes, I want to be sure to make the most of them. Store tomatoes properly, and they'll not only taste better but last longer too. Eat fresh tomatoes to your heart's desire, but remember that there are countless other ways to enjoy the incomparable taste of home-grown tomatoes year-round.

## HOW TO STORE TOMATOES

- Most vegetables last longer if kept in the refrigerator but tomatoes are an exception. Never store tomatoes in the refrigerator! It's a common mistake made by both gardeners and chefs. Cool temperatures actually cause tomatoes to lose flavour and become mealy-textured.

- If you like tomatoes chilled, put them in the refrigerator no more than an hour before serving.

- For tips on storing and ripening green tomatoes, see page 136.

Tomatoes with stems attached lose moisture more slowly and keep fresh longer than those with stems removed.

# GENERAL PROCEDURES FOR PRESERVING

- Examine jars; discard any with nicks or sharp edges on the rim that might prevent a good seal. Wash jars, rubber rings, glass lids and metal screw-bands in hot, soapy water.

- Sterilize jars by inverting them in several inches of simmering water for 20 minutes; cover. Leave jars in the hot water until just prior to filling. Sterilize lids and rubber rings according to manufacturer's directions.

*Using a boiling water bath canner to process home-canned tomatoes is essential to prevent food poisoning*

- If you are using jars with glass lids and separate rubber rings, always use **new** rubber rings.

- If you are using jars that have metal lids with an attached, rubber-like sealing compound, use a **new** lid each time.

- Prepare only the amount of tomatoes or tomato product that can be processed in the boiling water bath at one time. (See 'How to Process in a Boiling Water Bath Canner' on page 140.)

- One by one, fill each hot, sterilized jar with tomato mixture, leaving a ½-inch (1 cm) of headspace.

- Work a narrow spatula or knife around inside edges of filled jars to remove trapped air bubbles. Be sure to carefully wipe rims of jars with a clean, damp cloth after filling to remove any food that might prevent a good seal.

- To secure jars with **glass lids**, place correct size of wet rubber ring flat on jar and put lid on top. Screw metal screw-band tightly, then turn back ¼ turn.

- To secure jars with **metal lids**, place wet metal lid on jar and tighten screw-metal band firmly but do not make it excessively tight.

The beauty of having lots of overripe tomatoes is that you can make the best chutneys, marmalades and ketchups. One of my favourite uses for overripe tomatoes is spicy spaghetti sauce.

# How to Process in a Boiling Water Bath Canner

Tomatoes have a pH value of about 4.6, which is the dividing line between high- and low-acid foods.

- You will need a canner with a tight-fitting lid, large enough to allow 2 inches (5 cm) of space between jars, and deep enough to allow 2 inches (5 cm) of water above jars. Canners come with racks that hold jars off the bottom, and handles for easy removal of boiling-hot jars.

- Fill the canner halfway with boiling water. Insert the filled and sealed jars, and add more boiling water to cover jars by 2 inches (5 cm). Pour water down the sides of the canner rather than directly onto jars.

- Put the lid on the canner. Begin counting the processing time as soon as the water reaches a rolling boil.

- Keep water boiling for the entire time. If necessary, add boiling water during processing to maintain the water level.

- After processing, **do not re-tighten screw-bands of jars with metal lids.** If you are using jars with **glass lids**, tighten screw-bands immediately after processing.

Before filling each jar with tomatoes, add 1 tbsp. lemon juice per pint (15 ml per 500 ml) and 2 tbsp. lemon juice per quart (25 ml per 950 ml). If you wish, add sugar to mellow lemon juice's sharp flavour. Dissolve sugar in a bit of boiling water before adding it to the jar. Use 1 tsp. of sugar per pint (5 ml per 500 ml) and 2 tsp. sugar per quart (10 ml per 950 ml).

- Place jars upright on racks or a folded towel to cool, allowing several inches between jars. Metal lids often make a pinging noise as they cool; this indicates a vacuum has formed and the jar is properly sealed.

- Leave jars undisturbed for 24 hours, then check lids. Metal lids properly sealed are concave in the centre. Push the lid in the centre. If it does not push down, the jar is sealed. If it pushes down but pops back up, the jar is not sealed. Test glass-top jars for seal by tilting each jar on its side. If jars leak, they are not sealed.

*Andre Lema's first attempt at canning tomatoes was a great success.*

- Any jars that are not properly sealed must be refrigerated and used within 3 to 4 days. Otherwise, transfer the contents to a suitable container and freeze, or reprocess the unsealed jars. To reprocess, repeat entire procedure above, starting with newly sterilized jars and new rubber rings or metal lids. Contents must be reheated to boiling before adding to jars.

## Safety Tips for Home-processed Tomatoes

- Proper processing of home-canned food is extremely important to prevent botulism, a potentially fatal type of food poisoning caused by toxins produced by the bacterium *Clostridium botulinum*. The toxins are destroyed by being boiled for 10 minutes, but their spores can still grow in jars of canned low-acid foods. The spores are extremely resistant to heat.

Because of their texture, frozen tomatoes are best used for cooking. Paste tomatoes tend to hold their shape after defrosting better than other types of tomatoes.

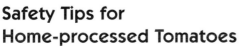 I never add spices to my canned tomato sauce until I am cooking. This way, I can take any of the stored jars, and use the sauce for pizza, spaghetti or other pastas, adding at the last minute whichever herbs and spices I like best for a particular dish.

If you like really thick sauce, boil whole tomatoes for 5 minutes and *then* chop them. This prevents the breakdown of pectin, which begins when tomatoes are sliced at room temperature. The more pectin breaks down, the less thick the sauce.

- To prevent food poisoning, you must add lemon juice to home-canned tomatoes that are processed in a boiling water bath. This increases acidity to a level that ensures safe preservation.

- If you like the flavour of olive oil in tomato sauce, wait to add it until you are ready to use the sauce in a recipe—unless you are using a pressure canner. To prevent botulism, a pressure canner must be used for tomato sauces made with olive oil—they cannot be safely processed in a boiling water bath.

- Tomatoes mixed with meat and lots of vegetables, such as stewed tomatoes or sauces, must also be processed only in a pressure canner. A boiling water bath does not reach high enough temperatures to eliminate possible bacterial contamination.

- Store jars of home-canned food products in a cool, dry place. Use within one year. Be sure to label and date your jars.

# WHAT TO DO WITH YOUR TOMATOES
## How to Can Tomatoes

*Paste tomatoes make the thickest sauce because they have more pectin than slicing tomatoes.*

- Wash tomatoes and blanch for one minute. Dip in cold water and remove skins. Remove core. Cherry tomatoes may be canned whole, with skins on.

- Add recommended amount of lemon juice to each jar (see page 140).

*Remember to sterilize jars and other equipment before you begin processing tomatoes.*

*There is absolutely no comparison between the taste of home-canned tomatoes and the tinned tomatoes from the store.*

- Tomatoes may be whole, halved or quartered. Pack raw tomatoes into hot, sterilized jars, pressing tomatoes down gently with a spatula to fill space and remove air pockets.

- Cover with boiling tomato juice, either commercial or home-made. Leave ½ inch (1 cm) headspace in each jar. For pint jars, you'll need ½–¾ cup (125–200 ml) of tomato juice, and for quart jars, 1–1 ½ cups (250 375 ml) of tomato juice. Secure lids as recommended above.

Process in a boiling water bath:

- whole tomatoes 50 minutes for pints and 60 minutes for quarts.

- quartered tomatoes 45 minutes for pints and 55 minutes for quarts.

# How to Make Tomato Juice
## QUICK TOMATO JUICE

- Put red, ripe, juicy tomatoes through a juicer, season with a pinch of sugar, salt, freshly ground pepper and a bit of lemon juice. Drink immediately.

## CANNED TOMATO JUICE

- Wash well-ripened tomatoes. Core and chop into small pieces.

- Boil 5 minutes in a large, covered pot.

- Pour through sieve; discard pulp and seeds. Return juice to the pot and bring to boil.

- Add recommended amount of lemon juice to hot, sterilized jars.

- Pour boiling-hot liquid into jars, leaving ½ inch (1 cm) headspace. Seal and process both pints and quarts for 45 minutes in a boiling water bath.

 For a low-fat, low-calorie meal, use tomato juice as a flavourful substitute to sauté onions and garlic for a rice or lentil dish.

*Home made tomato juice makes a delicious drink.*

## SPICED TOMATO JUICE

My son Bill's favourite juice is tomato. He likes tomato juice best when it's spiced up with ½ tsp. (2 ml ) **each** of Worcestershire and Tabasco sauce, some freshly ground black pepper and a bit of salt.

For those who like tomato juice with added zip, here are some tasty ideas:

- **Royale:** Blend 2 watercress sprigs, a dash of Worcestershire sauce, a pinch of pepper and 8 oz. (250 ml) tomato juice.

- **Southern Belle:** Blend 1 green pepper strip, dash each fresh lime juice and Tabasco sauce, ½ clove garlic, pinch of salt and pepper and 8 oz. (250 ml) tomato juice.

- **Fiesta:** Blend 3 fresh basil leaves, 1 thin onion slice, ½ clove garlic, ½ tsp. (2 ml) fresh lemon juice, pinch of salt and pepper and 8 oz. (250 ml) tomato juice.

- **El Greco:** Blend 4 thin, peeled cucumber slices, 1 thin onion slice, a small dill sprig and 8 oz. (250 ml) tomato juice.

- **Catalina:** Blend ½ cup (125 ml) sliced carrots, 1 parsley sprig, 1 tbsp. (15 ml) fresh lemon juice, dash Worcestershire sauce, pinch of salt and pepper and 8 oz. (250 ml) tomato juice.

## How to Make Tomato Sauce

- Wash well-ripened tomatoes. Core and chop into small pieces.

- Boil 5 minutes in a large, covered pot.

- Pour through sieve; discard pulp and seeds. Return sauce to pot and boil gently, uncovered, for about an hour or until thickened. Stir frequently to prevent sticking.

- Add recommended amount of lemon juice to hot sterilized jars (see page 140).

- Pour boiling-hot sauce into jars, leaving ½ inch (1 cm) headspace. Seal and process in a boiling water bath: pints for 50 minutes and quarts for 55 minutes.

To freeze cherry tomatoes, lay whole, washed tomatoes on a baking sheet. Place in freezer for several hours until frozen. Remove and put into plastic freezer bags or other suitable container. This method preserves their shape and prevents squashing. Skins will slip off when thawed.

## My Favourite Tomato Is...

'Champion is an all-around great variety:
good size, excellent juice and tender skin—
Champion has it all.'

*Jim Nau, New Variety and Trials Manager
West, Ball Seed Co., Chicago, Illinois*

## How to Freeze Tomatoes

### FREEZING WHOLE TOMATOES

* Wash, cover with boiling water and let stand 2–3 minutes. Drain. Pour cold water over top to cool.

* Remove skins and core; chop into pieces, if desired.

* Package and freeze.

* Option: Before freezing, cover with tomato juice, either commercial or home made, to improve colour and flavour.

### FREEZING TOMATO JUICE

* Wash, core and cut tomatoes into pieces.

* Place in pot and boil gently 2–3 minutes. Strain.

* Cool and pour into freezer containers, leaving 1 inch (2.5 cm) headspace. Freeze.

I usually freeze whole tomatoes without blanching or skinning—the skins will just slip off later during cooking.

*Many people consider a steaming bowl of canned tomato soup, made with milk and topped with crumbled saltine crackers, as 'comfort food,' something that stirs warm and reassuring memories of childhood days. Top soup company Campbell's has sold over 20 billion cans of tomato soup—about 4 cans for every person on the face of the earth. Tomato soup was Campbell's first product and 125 years later, still remains its all-time best-selling soup.*

## FREEZING TOMATO SAUCE

- Wash tomatoes, cover with boiling water and let stand 2–3 minutes. Drain. Pour cold water over top to cool.

- Remove skins and core. Cut into pieces and place in Dutch oven. Boil gently, uncovered, for about an hour or until thickened. Stir to prevent sticking.

- Place in blender or food processor. Blend.

- Strain, if desired, to remove seeds.

- Cool, pack and freeze.

- Option: For more flavour, add onion and green peppers to tomatoes while cooking.

*Use frozen tomato products within 8 months. Remember to label and date your containers.*

## FREEZING STEWED TOMATOES

- Wash tomatoes, cover with boiling water and let stand 2–3 minutes. Drain. Pour cold water over top to cool.

- Remove skins and core. Cut into pieces, if desired. Simmer in a large pot for 10–20 minutes.

- Cool, pack and freeze.

- Option: For variety, add celery, onion and green pepper to tomatoes while cooking.

## RICH TOMATO FREEZER SAUCE

12 tomatoes, cut into chunks

2 cups (500 ml) chopped onion

2 tbsp. (25 ml) oil

2 tbsp. (25 ml) red wine vinegar

½ tsp. (2 ml) sugar

In a large saucepan, sauté onion until soft. Add remaining ingredients and simmer, covered, 30–40 minutes, stirring occasionally to prevent scorching. Cool sauce and purée in blender or food processor. Pack into freezer containers and freeze. Yield: 1.5 litres.

*To easily peel skins from ripe tomatoes, place them into a bowl and pour boiling water over top to completely cover them. Leave for one minute, drain and run under cold water. The skins will split and slide off effortlessly. The riper the tomatoes, the better this method works.*

# How to Dry Tomatoes

*Allow about 15 pounds of fresh tomatoes to make 1 pound of dried tomatoes (6.8 kg fresh = 454 g dried).*

So-called 'sun-dried' tomatoes are often dried by means other than the sun. In my area, we seldom have the three- to four-day stretch of unbroken dry heat that's necessary for drying tomatoes outdoors. Oven-dried tomatoes are very good and easy to make— nothing is added, and only water is removed. Paste tomatoes are the best type for drying.

- Choose only fresh, ripe, unblemished tomatoes. Place into a bowl; pour boiling water over top to completely cover. Leave one minute, drain and run under cold water. The skins will split and slip off. Cut tomatoes in half, lengthwise.

- Begin drying immediately. Remove excess moisture with paper towels and arrange tomato slices, cut-side up, in a single layer on a baking tray.

**You can dry tomatoes in an oven...**

- Heat to 140°F (60°C) and prop door open for air circulation. Place tray on top rack in oven.

- Place tray of tomato slices into oven, positioning to allow air circulation. Turn over occasionally and rotate tray positions.

- It takes up to 24 hours to completely dry tomatoes. Drying times vary with the size and moisture content of tomato slices, the amount on the tray, and humidity. **Dry thoroughly**—remaining moisture will cause food to mould. Properly dried tomatoes are flexible and leathery.

- Remove dried tomatoes from oven and let stand at room temperature until cool.

Pound for pound, dried tomatoes have a higher than usual concentration of nutrients, especially minerals. Much vitamin A and C, however, is lost in the drying process.

**Or you can dry tomatoes in a food dehydrator ...**

- Follow manufacturer's directions. Tomatoes dry more quickly and evenly in a food dehydrator than in an oven, and they will retain more flavour and nutrients.

Place dried tomatoes into airtight containers or freezer bags. Store in a cool, dry, dark location. Dried tomatoes can be frozen.

Check containers after 24 hours for any signs of moisture. If you find moisture, return the tomatoes to the oven or dehydrator for further drying.

*Drying preserves food by removing enough moisture to prevent the growth of spoilage organisms.*

# SEVEN THINGS YOU NEVER KNEW ABOUT KETCHUP

1) The tomato sauce we now know as ketchup originates from a tangy Chinese concoction called *ketsiap*, developed in the 17th century and composed of fish entrails, vinegar and spices. The Chinese exported it to Malaya, where it was called *kechap*, and eventually sold to British sailors in the early 18th century. British cooks substituted mushrooms for fish entrails.

2) Although today we would be surprised if ketchup was not tomato-based, in the 19th century, tomato ketchup was not popular because many North Americans thought the plant was poisonous. Walnut, oyster, mushroom, lemon and anchovy were more-favoured ketchup varieties.

3) One of the first known ketchup recipes was published in 1812 under the title 'Tomate or Love-Apple Catsup.'

4) Originally, ketchup's claim to fame was its long storage life, purportedly lasting a sea voyage from England to India. According to *The Tomato in America*, some cookbook authors claimed their ketchup would keep for up to 20 years!

5) Ketchup used to be so highly valued that an 1836 inventory of an American senator's estate included...18 bottles of ketchup.

6) During the late 1800s, coal tar was used in some commercial ketchups to create an 'appealing' bright red colour.

*Paste tomatoes make the thickest sauces because they have a higher pectin content than other types of tomatoes. They are also slightly more acidic. Slicing tomatoes can also be used for sauces, but they have more juice to cook down and will not give the same thick texture as paste tomatoes.*

7) Catsup or ketchup? Originally, Henry Heinz used both spellings, but eventually settled on 'ketchup' when he began advertising his product in the early 1900s, reportedly because he liked the unique spelling. It wasn't until about 60 years later that his major competitor, J.W. Hunt, also switched from 'catsup' to 'ketchup.' Del Monte didn't change over until 1988.

## Old-fashioned Tomato Ketchup

18 cups ripe tomatoes, cut into quarters (approximately 8 lbs.)

1 ½ cups sliced onions (approximately 3 medium)

1 cup cider vinegar

¼ cup pickling salt

½ tsp. cayenne

1 ½ tsp. dry mustard

1 ½ cups brown sugar

1 ½ inch cinnamon stick

1 ½ tsp. whole cloves

1 ½ tsp. whole allspice

Cook onions and tomatoes until soft, approximately 20 minutes. Press through a coarse sieve, add remaining ingredients, tying whole spices loosely in a cheesecloth bag. Boil 1 ½ hours. Pour into hot, sterilized jars and seal. Process in a boiling water bath for 15 minutes. Yield: 3 ½ pints.

If you spill tomato juice or sauce on your carpet, the best way to remove the stain is with lots of water, non bleach detergent, more water, vinegar and more water.

# HERBS & TOMATOES

### *'...enhancing that tomato flavour...'*

*Don't be afraid to experiment with different herbs when preparing tomato dishes. Not all herbs complement tomatoes, but there are at least a dozen which are absolutely wonderful for enhancing tomato flavour. My favourites are oregano and basil. Other herbs that are excellent with tomatoes include bay leaf, chervil, chives, coriander, dill, garlic, lovage, marjoram, mint, parsley, rosemary, sage, savoury, tarragon and thyme.*

## GROWING HERBS WITH TOMATOES

- When I grow tomatoes in containers, I like to add a few herbs. I plant tall herbs like chives and some types of mint toward the back, and add trailing herbs such as oregano, marjoram and thyme in the front.

- Basil and tomatoes are natural companions in the kitchen, but they do not grow well planted in the same pot. I never plant them together because basil needs less water than tomatoes but lots of sun, and overhanging tomato leaves cause too much shade. Basil grows best in its own pot, put outdoors in late spring. You can plant tomatoes outside much earlier than basil.

Broiled herb tomatoes make a delicious quick snack or meal. To prepare, cut 4 large tomatoes in half across the middle, and place cut-side-up on a baking sheet. Mix ¼ cup dried bread crumbs with 1 tbsp. fresh herbs such as basil or oregano, ¼ cup freshly grated Parmesan cheese, and salt and pepper to taste. Sprinkle over top of tomato halves. Broil for 5 minutes, taking care not to burn. Serve immediately.

# Tomato & Herb Salad Dressing

Blue Flame Kitchen

175 ml tomato juice
50 ml red wine vinegar
15 ml chopped fresh parsley
1 ml salt
15 ml chopped green onion or chives
Dash each savoury, oregano, cayenne pepper,
    black pepper, garlic powder and sugar
15 ml oil, optional

Combine all ingredients. Cover and refrigerate up to 4 days.
Yield: 250 ml.

Either fresh or dried herbs can be used in most recipes. With fresh herbs, add about three times more than dried.

*For a colourful display, add a ring of marigolds around potted tomatoes, and tuck a few herbs, such as sage, marjoram or mint, into the planter.*

# NUTRITIOUS, DELICIOUS TOMATOES

*'...among the top nutrition picks...'*

*'Eat your vegetables' are well-known words of wisdom attributed to parents everywhere. You've probably also heard that 'parents know best,' and in this case, it is true. Vegetables are good for you, particularly if they are fresh. The fresher the vegetable, the more nutrition it packs into every mouthful. A freshly picked, vine-ripened tomato may have up to three times the vitamin C of a supermarket tomato.* Canada's Guide to Healthy Eating *and the National Cancer Institute both recommend eating at least four to five servings of vegetables or fruit each day. Obviously, some are better for you than others. Tomatoes are listed among the top nutrition picks by the* American Journal of Public Health.

*'Tomatoes, lettuce, carrots and peas,*

*Your mother says eat a lot of these.'*
*- ANON.*

# HOW GOOD ARE THEY?

- Tomatoes are low in fat and sodium, contain fibre and are high in potassium, phosphorous and vitamins A and C.

- One medium tomato provides more than half of the adult recommended daily allowance (RDA) of vitamin C and almost one-third the adult RDA of vitamin A, with only 25 calories.

Eating lots of raw tomatoes may significantly reduce the risk of certain types of cancer, according to a 1994 report in the *International Journal of Cancer*. Researchers believe that this might be due to a type of carotene called lycopene, an anti-oxidant that gives tomatoes their red colour. If this is true, cooked tomatoes may also offer protection because lycopene is not destroyed by heat.

'It takes roughly 300 cherry tomatoes to equal the calories in one chocolate ice-cream cone.'
- Jim Waltrip, Director of Wholesale, Petoseed, Saticoy, California (the world's largest producer of tomato seed).

*Juggling well-rounded meals with a busy life-style can be difficult, but the versatile tomato adds an easy balance of nutrition, low calories and mouth-watering flavour to almost any meal.*

# THE TOP TEN LIST OF NUTRITIOUS TOMATOES

 Vitamin A is not destroyed at ordinary cooking temperatures, but heating and oxidation does destroy vitamin C.

1) Orange tomatoes have the highest vitamin A content.

2) Ounce for ounce, cherry tomatoes have twice the vitamin C of larger tomatoes.

3) The most vitamin C is found in the gel around the seeds.

4) The riper the tomato, the more nutritious it is. Fresh red tomatoes contain almost four times the vitamin A of fresh green tomatoes.

5) The more sun the tomato plant gets while growing, the more vitamin C its fruit will contain.

6) Vine-ripened tomatoes have more nutrients than tomatoes that are picked green and shipped to stores.

7) Hothouse tomatoes from the grocery store have about the same amount of vitamin C as summer-grown field tomatoes. Field tomatoes that are picked green have less vitamin C and about half the vitamin A.

'A medium tomato has about as much fiber as a slice of whole-wheat bread.'
—*Food Lover's Companion*

8) Uncooked tomatoes have more vitamin C than cooked tomatoes.

9) Tomato paste contains more vitamins than tomato sauce.

10) Unpeeled tomatoes have slightly more vitamins than peeled tomatoes.

## My Favourite Tomato Is...

' Ultra sweet is a great-looking tomato, and it's good to the very last slice. Its great taste has been recognized by organic growers and by some of North America's top chefs.

—*Wayne Gale, General Manager, Stokes Seeds Ltd. St. Catharines, Ontario.*

# TOMATO MANIA

A 7-FOOT-TALL (2.15 m) tomato has taken on the job of promoting the city of Sacramento, California. The Big Tomato mascot is the creation of The Original Tomato Company.

THIS IS NOTHING, however, compared to the annual mass madness that occurs every August 30 in the Spanish town of Buñol during *La Tomatina*. Last year, about 20,000 people—twice as many as actually live in this town—transformed the main square into a red, juicy pool by throwing close to 100 tons (90.7 tonnes) of overripe tomatoes at each other. This festival honours San Luis, the town's patron saint, and dates back to the Middle Ages.

# APPENDIX
## Common Tomato Problems

At our garden centre, where staff assists gardeners in solving all sorts of plant-related problems, the same questions arise time after time. Have a look at the problems most commonly encountered with growing tomatoes, to avoid making these mistakes yourself.

# THE FOUR MOST COMMON SEEDING PROBLEMS

### 1) Raising seedlings too warm

This is the number one problem with home-grown tomato seedlings. Young plants grow best between 21 and 24°C (70–75°F)—average room temperature is fine. Above 27°C (80°F), you'll have tall, pale seedlings with weak, spindly growth. Within days, they will flop over and often will die. The problem is usually caused by failure to remove the seedling flat from the source of bottom heat *as soon as* seedlings begin to emerge. The lack of light inside most homes makes seedlings even more susceptible.

### 2) Sowing too early

When you sow seeds too early, the seedlings become tall and 'stretched' in their efforts to find sufficient light inside your home. This results in weakened plants that, when transplanted into the garden, will be more susceptible to all sorts of problems and generally just won't grow as well. For best results, wait to sow tomatoes until five to six weeks before transplanting them outdoors.

### 3) Sowing too shallow

If seed is not sown deep enough, the seedlings will grow out of the seedling mix, resulting in their being injured or dying. Try gently pressing the seedlings back into the seedling mix, and cover with a bit more fine vermiculite. In future, prevent this problem by gently pressing seed into the soil mix before covering with vermiculite.

### 4) Sowing too thick

Sowing too thick results in weak, spindly, crowded seedlings, and there is a greater chance of root damage when transplanting. If your seedlings are too crowded, sacrifice a few to save the rest. Next time, try to sow so that thinning is not required. Ideally, tomato seedlings should be as wide as or wider than they are tall.

Do not leave dead tomato vines in the garden at the end of the season, because they provide a perfect place for pests to overwinter. Till them into soil, or chop them up and compost them.

*Leaf roll (left) is normal and nothing to worry about, but 2,4-D damage (above) can kill tomato plants.*

# THE MOST COMMON LEAF PROBLEMS

*The leaves on my tomato plants are twisted and deformed, and the plants are not growing well.*

There are two possibilities:

1) If the damage is predominately on new growth, the most common cause is that they have inadvertently been sprayed with 2,4-D or similar weed-killers. New growth is affected first, but older leaves may also become twisted, curled or deformed. Spray from lawn weed-killers can drift a fair distance, so never apply weed-killers on a windy day, nor anywhere near tomato plants. Tomato plants with 2,4-D damage can't be saved and should be thrown out.

2) Curled older leaves, commonly called 'leaf roll,' can happen after periods of heavy rain, or when there is a wide variation between day and night temperatures. Certain varieties are more susceptible than others, but leaf roll does not harm plants.

   If curled or rolled-up leaves are the only symptom, and the plants otherwise seem fine, free of disease and pests, do not worry about it. Watering regularly, evenly and thoroughly, planting in rich, well-drained soil and growing hybrid varieties help to lessen leaf roll.

### Why do the lower leaves on my tomato plants turn yellow?

There are a few possibilities, but this is usually nothing to worry about—it's most often merely due to age. Older leaves become less productive as they age and should be removed.

Yellow lower leaves could also, however, be caused by a nitrogen deficiency. Nitrogen is highly mobile in plants, resulting in it moving to young growing parts like new leaves and shoots, and abandoning the old tissue. For recommendations on fertilizing, see pages 110–113.

If the leaves are wilted, there are brown streaks up stems and the entire plant is less vigorous or suddenly collapses, the problem may be some type of root-rot. If possible, improve drainage immediately to try to save the plant—for example, remove saucers underneath containers and ensure that there are sufficient drainage holes, because roots sitting in water suffocate and rot. In future, avoid root-rot by choosing resistant varieties (ones listed with the letters 'V' and 'F'—see page 166 for a more detailed description). If planting in containers, ensure containers are sterile; if planting in the garden, try a new location. In either case, plant in soil that will drain well.

### My plants have greyish-white patches on the fruit and leaves.

This is likely 'sun-scald,' which is caused by excessive or sudden exposure to intense sunlight and heat. Before planting seedlings you have raised in your home, acclimatize them to the more intense light outdoors (see page 33). Plant tomatoes away from white, sun-reflecting walls or cover those walls with a non-reflective covering, such as burlap. Do not remove leaves that are protecting fruit from direct sunlight.

*Early blight affects lower, older leaves first.*

### What causes the blotches on leaves when tomato plants are growing rapidly?

This may be due to early blight, which typically first affects older leaves closest to the ground and then moves upwards, causing younger leaves to die and drop, and eventually affecting the entire plant. Prune off infected leaves or destroy badly infected plants. Do not compost these plants; disease spores can overwinter. Plant resistant varieties in good soil (which reduces severity) and fertilize regularly. Avoid wetting the foliage when watering. Early blight is most prevalent in humid regions or semi-arid areas with frequent dews.

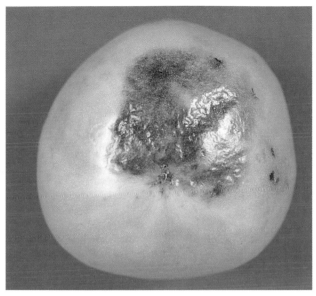

*Late blight is the same fungal disease that caused the Irish potato famine in the 1840s.*

Late blight attacks all the above-ground parts of the tomato. It begins as leaf spots and spreads to stems and fruit. It is most serious during consistently cool, rainy weather, or when nights are cool and daytime temperatures are below 30°C (86°F). Spores spread rapidly by wind and can travel 200 miles (322 km) in the air. Late blight is not a problem in cooler climates, but it is a severe problem in many areas of the U.S. and Mexico. There is no cure but there are preventive sprays, and plant breeders are now trying to develop resistant varieties. Gardeners in susceptible areas should check with local garden centres for recommended preventive measures.

### My leaves look fine, but there are a lot of little white insects that fly up from my tomato plants. Should I worry about them?

That sounds like whitefly, mainly a greenhouse problem in my area, but also a garden problem in more southern areas. Whiteflies cause little damage in small numbers but can multiply rapidly in warm temperatures and then cause serious damage. The main problem with whiteflies is they secrete a honeydew on fruit and foliage that a fungus called 'sooty mould' grows upon. Sooty mould can rapidly cover tomatoes, severely affecting plant growth.

In our greenhouse, we use sticky, yellow paper traps to monitor whitefly. As soon as we find even one, it's time to start spraying with insecticidal soap. Thorough coverage of each plant is essential! Repeat every

Do not plant vegetables of the same family together, because they attract the same pests. Separating your tomatoes from peppers, eggplants and potatoes makes it harder for pests to spread from one to the other.

four to five days, up to four or five times. If one plant is badly infested, the best solution is to get rid of it in order to save the others.

The best solution for whitefly is prevention. Keep greenhouses really clean. Whiteflies are attracted to many plants other than tomatoes, including weeds, so be vigilant and remove all weeds inside and around your garden or greenhouse.

### How do I get rid of aphids?

Aphids are small, soft-bodied insects that mainly affect new growth. If the infestation is bad, older growth will also be affected and a sooty mould can grow on aphid secretions on leaves and fruit. You do not have to eliminate every single aphid, but merely control their numbers. Insecticidal soaps work well and are safe to use on vegetables. Ladybugs feed on aphids. Some garden centres sell lures to attract ladybugs to your garden, and also sell boxes full of live ladybugs!

### What causes the small 'shot holes' in leaves?

Usually this is caused by flea beetles, which are tiny dark beetles that jump like fleas and chew small round holes in leaves. The damage is mostly cosmetic, so you needn't worry about it. Alternatively, dust with rotenone (an insecticide derived from the roots of tropical plants).

*Aphids can be controlled using insecticidal soaps or soapy water, but be sure not to use detergent or you may kill your plants.*

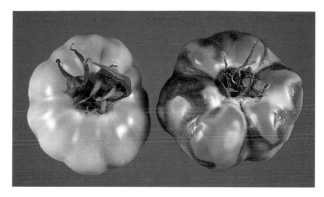

*The organisms that cause tobacco mosaic virus (TMV) can live for 50 years if kept dry, survive temperatures of 120°C (248°F) for 30 minutes, and cause infection at a dilution of one part per million in the plant's sap.*

**The upper leaves on my tomato plant are thin and rolled up, like shoestrings. What causes this?**

The distinctive 'shoestring' leaves are a symptom of tobacco mosaic virus (TMV). Plants will become stunted and fruit may be affected. Throw out infected plants—there is no cure. Smokers should wash their hands before handling tomato plants to avoid passing on this disease. Many hybrid varieties have inbred resistance.

# THE MOST COMMON FRUIT PROBLEMS

**Why are my ripe or ripening tomatoes cracking on the vine?**

These 'growth cracks' are caused by very rapid growth, often during a warm, rainy period following a dry spell, especially when fruit is full-sized and beginning to turn red. Certain varieties are more susceptible to cracking than others. Keep moisture supply as even as possible through-out the season.

**There are unusual swellings and scar-like streaks on my tomatoes.**

This is called 'cat-facing,' a condition resulting from abnormal flower development, caused by unusually hot or cool weather during pollina-tion. The tomatoes are less attractive but still edible.

*Tomatoes with growth cracks, although less attractive, are still fine for eating.*

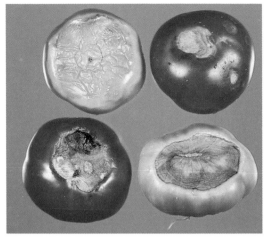

### What causes black or brown rotten spots on the bottom of tomatoes?

This is a condition called 'blossom-end rot,' caused by water stress or calcium deficiency due to poor or heavy clay soils, or irregular or inadequate watering, especially during a period of rapid growth. Improve watering practices to save developing fruit.

*If your tomatoes develop blossom-end rot, cut off the affected portions; the remainder of the tomato is fine for eating.*

Watering regularly and evenly is the key to preventing blossom-end rot. Even if soil contains lots of calcium, without sufficient water, the plants cannot absorb the calcium.

There is a calcium-chloride spray that you can buy to reduce problems with blossom-end rot, but this will not be necessary if you plant in rich soil, feed with a balanced fertilizer containing calcium, and water properly. Some hybrid varieties have an inbred resistance to blossom-end rot.

### What are the small black spots on my tomatoes?

This is likely 'bacterial speck,' a disease that is typically spread from infected soil splashing onto the fruit and foliage during a heavy rainfall. Attach a soft-rain nozzle to your hose to prevent splashing foliage while you are watering. If the infected plant is an heirloom variety from which you want to save seed, be sure to use a hot-water treatment to disinfect the seed. Store as you would normally, but next spring, just before planting, cover seed with hot water (50°C/122°F). Leave for 25 minutes, then remove seed from water and spread out to dry on a glass or ceramic dish. (See 'How to Save Tomato Seed' on page 132 for details on saving seed.)

### Why are this year's tomato plants bearing very few fruit while last year's plants produced well?

There are several possible reasons, including the three most common: not enough sun, too much nitrogen, and low temperatures during pollination.

**1) Not enough sun**

Tomato plants do best in a very sunny location. With less light, you will still get fruit but there will be fewer, and they will not taste as good as those grown in sunnier spots. Sometimes gardeners tell me that they have grown the same tomatoes in the same vegetable garden for years, but production is dropping each year. What they may not be taking into consideration is how much more shade there is as the trees in their yard mature. In this situation, I suggest growing tomatoes in containers, which can easily be placed in a sunnier location.

## 2) Too much nitrogen

If your plants have enough sunlight but still produce few tomatoes, it may be because you are using the wrong fertilizer. Different plants have different nutrient needs, which is why there are so many kinds of fertilizer. A lawn fertilizer, for example, may contain five times the level of nitrogen as that needed by tomato plants. With tomatoes, too much nitrogen results in dark green, leafy plants but very few fruit. Fresh manure can have the same effect. Use a fertilizer that is recommended for tomatoes.

## 3) Sudden cold temperatures during blooming

Cool, cloudy weather or a sudden drop in temperature when plants are blossoming can adversely affect pollination. Low overnight temperatures cause the blossoms of some varieties to drop. Curiously enough, some of the varieties that do best in cool temperatures also do very well in extremely hot conditions.

There is a fruit-set spray that can be used in cooler temperatures to prevent fruit from dropping. It works by sealing the joint at the 'knuckle,' on the stem just above the fruit. I rarely use this, but instead depend on varieties such as Northern Exposure, which has the ability to pollinate well despite persistent cool temperatures.

## 4) Variety

If you are growing a different variety this year, maybe it is one that just has poor yields. Some of the older varieties produce far fewer fruit than the newer hybrids. Low fruit production can also result from growing a variety that matures too late for your area.

*Bacterial speck is a soil-borne disease that thankfully is not terribly common.*

### 5) Pruning

If you prune a determinate variety, you will greatly lower its yields. If you don't prune an indeterminate variety, yields may be slightly lower. By incorrectly pruning an indeterminate variety, you may be removing or breaking off flower clusters, resulting in fewer fruit.

### 6) Lack of moisture

Parched plants will be stunted and have fewer fruit. Water properly to prevent this.

# WEATHER-RELATED PROBLEMS

*My plants were damaged but not killed by frost. What should I do?*

If small tomato plants are damaged by frost early in the season, the best solution is to replace them with new plants. The damaged plants may still grow, but will be set so far back that they may not mature by the end of the growing season.

If frost occurs later in the season, salvage plants that are not too badly damaged. Leave them alone for a couple of days, then prune off affected leaves. Give plants a boost with a shot of fertilizer and follow up with lots of water to promote new growth. The fruit can take a little more cold than the leaves and may be okay. Frost-damaged fruit will be soft and not fit for eating.

*My plants were damaged by hail. What should I do?*

If all or most of the leaves were knocked off by hail, it is best to replant. With plants that were not too badly damaged, leave them alone for a couple of days, then prune off  affected leaves. Fertilize and water heavily.

Tomato hornworms are green caterpillars that eat mostly leaves, not actual tomatoes, and are so-named for the distinctive red spike or 'horn' that protrudes from one end. These caterpillars are not a problem in my area, but can be a terrible pest in most of the U.S. and southeastern Canada.  Despite the report quoted below, the truth is that tomato hornworms are harmless to humans.

Hand-picking is one method of controlling tomato hornworms, but if you see one with white, rice-like eggs on its back, let it be. Those eggs contain the larvae of parasitic wasps that feed on and kill tomato hornworms. The more eggs you allow to mature, the more wasps there will be to fight these green caterpillars.

---

'This worm was first discovered this season, and is poisonous as a rattlesnake. It poisons by throwing spittle, which it can throw from one to two feet. This spittle striking the skin, the parts commence at once to swell, and in a few hours death ends the agonies of the patient. Three cases of death in consequence of this poison have been reported. The medical profession is much excited over the new enemy to human existence.'

—a newspaper report from the 1860s on the tomato hornworm, cited in *The Tomato in America*

# ENLISTING MOTHER NATURE'S HELP

- 'Fight bugs with bugs' is the ecological approach taken by many greenhouse operators these days. They find that releasing minuscule (less than ⅛-inch [3 mm] long) predatory wasps called *Encarsia formosa* is effective in the battle against whitefly. At this stage, however, this is still a rather expensive solution, even for larger commercial greenhouses.

- In your garden, know which insects are the good guys. Ladybugs eat aphids, for example, and parasitic wasps kill tomato hornworms.

- A new hybrid tomato plant called 'Allure' lures Colorado potato beetles and aphids away from neighbouring plants. Allure, a stunted, rather ugly-looking plant with woolly, grey-green leaves that produces tomatoes too late in the season to be of use, was developed by Stokes Seeds of St. Catharines, Ontario. Stokes reports that a row of their Allure plants averaged about 12 beetles per plant for every one beetle per plant on a neighbouring row of tomato plants, and that insects continued to feed on Allure even after insecticides were applied to protect the plants.

We tried Allure last summer in a row of potatoes in our vegetable garden without much success, but it certainly warrants another try.

*Marigolds deter nematodes (thin-as-hair, worm-like organisms that attack roots), especially if planted for several seasons in the spot where nematodes were a problem. The best results were achieved when tomatoes were planted where an entire bed of marigolds had grown the previous year. Field studies in Zimbabwe successfully controlled five species of nematode, resulting in considerably fewer root knots and in heavier crops of tomatoes.*

*The hybrid tomato plant Allure attracts bugs, allowing you to control insects on that plant and avoid having to spray your whole crop.*

# DISEASE-RESISTANT VARIETIES

In all likelihood, you will never see the worst tomato diseases in your garden, because most hybrid varieties have been bred for resistance. Disease-resistance ratings are assigned after a dozen or more varieties growing side by side are saturated with disease organisms and then compared at weekly intervals. Those that show little or no infection are rated 'resistant' while those that show slightly more infection but still look pretty good are rated 'tolerant.' Don't assume that varieties without ratings are susceptible; they may just never have been tested.

Within the variety description, seed catalogues often list an abbreviation such as VF2NT or VFFN to indicate the variety's resistance to a particular disease. Here's how to decipher those abbreviations for tomatoes.

A: Alternaria stem canker, a fungal disease that infects tomatoes.

F, FF or F2: Fusarium wilt, a soil-borne fungus that attacks through roots and causes stems to rot at ground level. It reduces the plant's water intake to 2–4 per cent of normal, stunts plant growth and is worst in warm climates. FF or F2 indicates resistance to two different strains of this fungus.

N: Nematodes, thin, worm-like organisms that attack roots; most serious in southern regions; not actually a disease, but often listed with diseases because they cause similar symptoms in affected plants.

St: Stemphylium (grey leaf spot), a fungus that causes brownish-grey dead spots on foliage.

T or TMV: Tobacco mosaic virus, a viral disease transmitted from tobacco products or plants, usually by people.

V: Verticillium wilt, a common soil-borne fungal disease affecting the vascular system (the plant equivalent of human veins); prevents the movement of water and nutrients.

'A ripe, sun-warmed tomato that is picked off the vine and eaten right away will cause brain fever' —another unfounded myth about tomatoes.

| PROBLEM | LIKELY CAUSE | SOLUTION |
|---------|--------------|----------|
| Spindly growth | 1) Shade. 2) With seedlings, low light and excessive heat. | 1) If possible, increase the amount of light your plants receive in your present location, or move them to a sunnier site. 2) Cool seedlings after germination. Use grow lights. Refer to page 19. |
| Dwarf plants | Low fertility. | Feed plants with a balanced fertilizer, such as 20-20-20, to improve growth. |
| Purple leaves | Phosphorous deficiency. | Use a fertilizer with a high middle number, such as 10-52-10, every time you water. |
| Yellow leaves | Lack of nitrogen. | Feed plants with a balanced fertilizer, such as 20-20-20. Also see page 158. |
| Discoloured roots | High soil salts. | This is the most common in container gardens. Don't use fertilizer excessively. Never use fresh manure. |
| Spotted lower leaves | Magnesium deficiency. | Add Epsom salts to soil. Mix one tablespoon per gallon (15 ml per 4.5 litres) of water. Apply once every one or two weeks. |

# QUICK REFERENCE CHART

| VARIETY | TYPE | SIZE | DTM | RESISTANCE |
|---|---|---|---|---|
| **BEEFMASTER** | I - F1 | Huge | 80 days | **VFNASt, cracking** |
| *My biggest recommended beefsteak tomato.* | | | | |
| **BIG BEEF** | I - F1 | Extra-large | 73 days | **VFFNTASt** |
| *An impressive newcomer with many nicely shaped, flavourful, big tomatoes.* | | | | |
| **CELEBRITY** | D - F1 | Large | 72 days | **VFFNTASt, cracking, blight tolerant** |
| *A wonderful variety for home gardeners—lots of great-tasting tomatoes & no pruning.* | | | | |
| **CHAMPION** | I - F1 | Large | 62 days | **VFNT** |
| *Perfect for sandwiches.* | | | | |
| **COUNTER** | I - F1 | Medium | 60 days | **blossom-end rot** |
| *Beautiful—heavy yields of perfect, round tomatoes; great for both gardens & home greenhouses.* | | | | |
| **EARLY GIRL** | I - F1 | Medium | 52 days | **VFF, cracking** |
| *My earliest recommended slicing tomato. I think everyone should grow at least one Early Girl.* | | | | |
| **FLORAMERICA** | D - F1 | Large | 75 days | **VFFASt, blossom-end rot, blight tolerant** |
| *The best bush-type beefsteak—great for containers & my recommendation for farm women.* | | | | |
| **HEARTLAND** | S - F1 | Medium | 68 days | **VFN** |
| *The condo tomato, attractive in planters & flowerbeds.* | | | | |
| **LEMON BOY** | I - F1 | Medium | 72 days | **VFNASt** |
| *Lovely, lemon-yellow, a pleasing, mild flavour.* | | | | |
| **MAMMA MIA** | D - F1 | Paste | 62 days | **VFF** |
| *The highest-yielding paste tomato with triple the yields of most paste varieties.* | | | | |
| **NORTHERN EXPOSURE** | D - F1 | Large | 67 days | **VFFNTASt** |
| *Our most popular variety in 1995. Lots of big, tasty tomatoes; bred for short seasons & cooler temperatures.* | | | | |
| **SUNGOLD** | I - F1 | Cherry | 60 days | |
| *In my view, the best-tasting cherry tomato in the world!* | | | | |
| **SUPER FANTASTIC** | I - F1 | Large | 70 days | **VFN** |
| *The highest-yielding beefsteak tomato among my recommendations.* | | | | |
| **SWEET 100** | I - F1 | Cherry | 60 days | |
| *The highest-yielding cherry tomato I've grown.* | | | | |
| **TINY TIM** | D - OP | Cherry | 45 days | |
| *Ornamental dwarf variety ideal for children.* | | | | |
| **TUMBLER** | D - F1 | Small | 49 days | |
| *By far, the heaviest producer for size of plant; variety bred especially for hanging baskets & containers.* | | | | |
| **VENDOR** | I - OP | Greenhouse | 70 days | **VFT** |
| *One of the best-tasting greenhouse tomatoes.* | | | | |
| **WHOPPER (OG50)** | I - F1 | Extra-large | 65 days | **VFFNT, cracking, blossom-end rot** |
| *Outyields most older beefsteak varieties.* | | | | |

# SEED SOURCES

W. Atlee Burpee Co., 300 Park Avenue, Warminster, PA, 18991–0001, USA. Telephone: 1-800-888-1447 Fax: 1-800-487-5530

Heritage Seed Program, RR3, Uxbridge, ON, L9P 1R3, Canada. Telephone: (905) 623-0353

Holc's Greenhouses & Gardens Ltd., 101 Bellerose Drive, St. Albert, AB, T8N 8N8, Canada. Telephone: 1-800-459-6498 or Fax: (403) 459-6042

Johnny's Selected Seeds, Foss Hill Road, Albion, ME, 04910, USA. Telephone: (207) 437-4395 Fax: (207) 437-4290

Johnsons Seeds. London Road, Boston, Lincolnshire PE218AD England Telephone: (1205) 365-051 Fax: (1205) 310-148

McFayden Seed Co. Ltd., 30 - 9th Street, Suite 200, Brandon, MB, R7A 6N4, Canada. Telephone: (204) 725-7300, 1-800-205-7111 Fax: (204) 725-1888

Park Seed Co., Cokesbury Road, Greenwood, SC, 29647-0001, USA. Telephone: (803) 223-7333 Fax: (803) 941-4206

Seed Savers Exchange, 3076 N. Winn Road, Decorah, IA, 52101, USA. Telephone: (319) 382-5990 Fax: (319) 382-5872

Seeds of Change, P.O. Box 15700, Santa Fe, NM, 87506-5700, USA. Telephone: (505) 438-8080

Stokes Seeds Ltd., 39 James Street, Box 10, St. Catharines, ON, L2R 6R6, Canada. Telephone: (905) 688-4300 Fax: (905) 684-8411

Stokes Seeds Inc., Box 548, Buffalo, NY, 14240-0548, USA. Telephone: (716) 695-9649 Fax: (716) 695-6980

Territorial Seeds Co. (Canada) Ltd., 206 - 8475 Ontario Street, Vancouver, BC, V5X 3E8, Canada. Telephone: (604) 322-5266 Fax: (604) 322-5266

Territorial Seeds, P.O. Box 157, Cottage Grove, OR, 97424, USA. Telephone: (503) 942-9547 Fax: (503) 942-9881

Thompson & Morgan Inc., P.O. Box 1308, Jackson, NJ, 08527-0308, USA. Telephone: (908) 363-2225 Fax: (908) 363-9356

Tomato Growers Supply Company, P.O. Box 2237, Fort Myers, FL, 33902, USA. Telephone: (813) 768-1119 Fax: (813) 768-3476

Unwins Seed Limited, Histon, Cambridge CB44LE England Telephone (1223) 236-236 Fax: (1223) 237-437

Vesey's Seeds Ltd., Box 9000, Charlottetown, PE, C1A 8K6, Canada. Telephone: 1-800-363-7333, (902) 368-7333 Fax: (902) 566-1620

## KEY TO ABBREVIATIONS

DTM = days to maturity from transplanting
I = indeterminate
D = determinate
S= semi-determinate
F1 = hybrid
OP = open-pollinated
V = verticillium

F = fusarium
FF = two races of fusarium
N= nematodes
T = tobacco mosaic virus
A = alternaria
St = stemphylium

# BIBLIOGRAPHY

Ashworth, Suzanne. *Seed to Seed: Seed Saving Techniques for the Vegetable Gardener.* Decorah, IA: Seed Saver Publications, 1991.

Barrett, Judy. *Tomatillos: A Gardener's Dream, A Cook's Delight.* Georgetown, TX: AMS Publications, 1992.

Clement, Diane. *Diane Clement at the Tomato.* Vancouver, BC: Raincoast Books, 1995.

DuBose, Fred. *The Total Tomato.* New York: Harper & Row, Publishers Inc., 1985.

Gin, Margaret. *Tomatoes.* San Francisco: 101 Productions, 1977.

Herbst, Sharon Tyler. *The Food Lover's Companion.* Hauppauge, NY: Barron's Educational Series, Inc., 1990.

Mintzberg, Henry. *Mintzberg on Management: Inside Our Strange World of Organizations.* New York: Macmillan, Free Press, 1989.

Riotte, Louise. *Carrots Love Tomatoes: Secrets of Companion Planting for Successful Gardening.* Pownal, VT: Storey Communications, Inc., 1975.

Ritzler, Carol Ann. *The Complete Book of Food.* New York: World Almanac, 1987.

Schneider, Elizabeth. *Uncommon Fruits & Vegetables: A Commonsense Guide.* New York: Harper & Row, 1986.

Shenfield, Patti. *Flavors of Home: Creative Cooking from Down-Home to Gourmet.* Drayton Valley, AB: Palastair Enterprises, 1994.

Smith, Andrew F. *The Tomato in America: Early History, Culture, and Cookery.* Columbia, SC: University of South Carolina, 1994.

Staten, Vince. *Can You Trust a Tomato in January?: The Hidden Life of Groceries and Other Secrets of the Supermarket Revealed at Last.* New York: Simon & Schuster, 1993.

Stoll, Clifford. *Silicon Snake Oil: Second Thoughts on the Information Highway.* New York: Bantam Doubleday Dell Publishing Group, Inc., 1995.

## Magazines & Other Publications

Aylsworth, Jean D. "To Stake or Not to Stake." *American Vegetable Grower* 43, no. 8.

Cardillo, Rob. "Very Cherry Tomatoes." *Organic Gardening*, April 1995, 40-44.

*Edmonton Journal*, 23 August 1995.

*International Journal of Cancer* 59, 1994.

Land, Leslie. "Real Tomatoes." *Food & Wine*, August 1991, 49-54.

Meyer, Scott. "Pick No Produce Before Its Prime." *Organic Gardening,* September/October 1994.

————. "Twilight-Zone Tomatoes." *Organic Gardening,* March 1994, 38-44.

Moore, Jim. "DNAP's FreshWorld Nears Market with Genetic Tomato." *American Vegetable Grower,* December 1994.

Nardozzi, Charlie. "Serious About Sauce Tomatoes." *National Gardening* 16, no. 6, 40-41.

Ocone, Lynn. "America's Favorite Vegetables." *National Gardening,* January/February 1995.

*Off the Vine* newsletter, NY.

Pleasant, Barbara. "Secrets of Professional Pest Spotters." *Organic Gardening,* July/August 1995, 26-28.

Schultz, Judy. "Some Tomatoes." *Edmonton Journal,* 21 August 1991.

————. "Terrific Tomatoes." *Edmonton Journal,* 20 September 1995.

————. "The Highly Personal Pizza." *Edmonton Journal,* 6 August 1995.

*Small-Scale Agriculture Today* newsletter, US Department of Agriculture - Cooperative State Research. Education & Extension Service, Summer 1995, p. 3.

Stone, Pat. "Tomato Blight: An Interview with Randy Gardner." *National Gardening,* July/August 1995.

*Today's Garden* newsletter, National Garden Bureau, July 1994.

*The Avant Gardener* newsletter 27, Horticultural Data Processors, August 1995.

*The Tomato Club* newsletter. Bogota, NJ.

*UC Berkeley Wellness Letter,* University of California, March 1994.

Usher, Rod. "The Russians Are Coming Black." *Time,* May 15, 1995.

Vavrina, C.S. "Tomato Transplanting Reaches New Depths." *American Vegetable Grower* 43, no. 4.

Whysall, Steve. "Club plumps for tomatoes: 'the wondrous fruit'." *Vancouver Sun,* 8 July 1995.

————. "Nature's Debt Repaid." *The Globe & Mail Report on Business Magazine* 12, no. 3.

# Recommended Reading

*The Tomato Club,* 114 E. Main Street, Bogota, NJ, 07603. Telephone: (201) 488-2231. Fax: (201) 489-4609. Bi-monthly newsletter packed full of news, growing tips, helpful hints and humorous items. A "don't miss" read for the avid tomato grower!

*Tomatillos: A Gardener's Dream, A Cook's Delight.* Judy Barret. AMS Publications, P.O. Box 913, Georgetown, TX, 78627.

# SELECT INDEX

# CREDITS

Folklore from *Popular Beliefs and Superstitions: A Compendium of American Folklore*, copyright © 1981, Cleveland Public Library, John G. White Collection.

Information on saving seeds (p. 132) courtesy Seed Savers Exchange.

'The Tryst' and 'Ode to a Home-grown Tomato' courtesy of *The Tomato Club* newsletter.

## Recipes*

Recipes for Tomato Pizza and Marinated Salad adapted from the *Edmonton Journal*.

Recipe for Salsa Verde from *Tomatillos: A Gardener's Dream, A Cook's Delight* by Judy Barrett.

Recipe for Salsa Fresca adapted from the *Calgary Herald*.

Recipe for Salad of Avocado, Cape Gooseberries and Cucumber from *Uncommon Fruits & Vegetables: A Commonsense Guide* by Elizabeth Schneider. Copyright © 1986 by Elizabeth Schneider. Reprinted by permission of HarperCollins Publishers, Inc.

Recipes for BBQ Green Tomato Stir-Fry, Tomato & Herb Salad Dressing, Tomatoes Babiche, Old-fashioned Ketchup and procedures for storing, preserving and canning courtesy of the Blue Flame Kitchen, Northwestern Utilities Ltd.

Roast Beef recipe from *Traditional Jamaican Cookery* by Norma Benghiat (Penguin Books, 1985) copyright © Norma Benghiat 1985.

*In reprinting these recipes, we have retained as much as possible each cook's own style, organization and measurement preferences.

# ABOUT THE AUTHOR

Lois Hole and her husband Ted started selling vegetables out of their red barn more than 30 years ago; today, Hole's Greenhouse & Gardens Ltd. is one of the largest greenhouse and garden centres in Alberta. It remains a family business, owned and operated by Lois, Ted, their sons Bill and Jim, and Bill's wife Valerie.

Lois was born and raised in rural Saskatchewan, and later moved to Edmonton, Alberta. She attained a degree in Music from the Toronto Conservatory of Music.

Over the years, Lois has shared her expertise by writing gardening columns and speaking on radio shows and at various gardening functions. Her practical wisdom and sound advice were so much in demand that she decided to begin a series of gardening guides. The first three books in the series, *Vegetable Favorites*, *Bedding Plant Favorites* and *Perennial Favorites*, have all become bestsellers, and the Professional Plant Growers Association has recognized the series as an exceptional source of information by awarding it their Educational Media Award for 1995.

*Every year, Lois, her mother Elsa and Auntie Anne gather to preserve the season's bounty of tomatoes.*

 # Enjoy The Rest of Lois's Books!

## LOIS HOLE'S PERENNIAL FAVORITES
### *by Lois Hole with Jill Fallis*

Drawing on her 30 years' experience in gardening and operating a gardening center, Lois Hole has chosen 100 perennial plants for their beauty and hardiness. With common sense and practical wisdom, she tells you all you need to know to easily transform any patch of earth into a spectacular garden. More than 430 color photographs and lots of straight-forward tips, including flower colors, height ranges, blooming periods, planting strategies, and tips for solving common problems.

5.5" x 8.5" • 352 pages • over 430 color photographs • Softcover • $19.95 CDN $15.95 US • ISBN 1-55105-056-0

## LOIS HOLE'S BEDDING PLANT FAVORITES
### *by Lois Hole with Jill Fallis*

Turn your bare patch of soil into a glorious garden full of color with annual flowers and advice from Lois Hole, gardening expert and greenhouse operator. Written for anyone who likes to put plants into the earth, this book is full of ideas about how to make your favorite flowers thrive. Extend your garden into your home with flower drying, bouquet and fragrance ideas. Lois Hole doesn't expect you to be an expert; she offers good advice, not an encyclopedia.

5.5" x 8.5" • 272 pages • over 350 color photographs Softcover • $19.95 CDN • $15.95 US• ISBN 1-55105-039-0

## LOIS HOLE'S VEGETABLE FAVORITES
### *by Lois Hole*

With growing tips, variety recommendations, recipes and nutritional hints, Lois Hole describes how to grow, harvest and prepare more than 30 of her favorite vegetables. Suggestions for composting, fertilizing, pest control and small-space gardening make this colorful and inspirational guide a horn of plenty.

5.5" x 8.5" • 160 pages • 44 color photographs • 51 B & W illustrations • 33 color illustrations • Softcover • $14.95 CDN • $11.95 US ISBN 1-55105-029-0

## LONE PINE PUBLISHING
### PHONE
# 1-800-661-9017
### FAX
# 1-800-424-7173